Bookkeeping Basics
What Every Nonprofit Bookkeeper Needs to Know

by Debra L. Ruegg and Lisa M. Venkatrathnam
LarsonAllen Public Service Group

AMHERST H.
WILDER
FOUNDATION

SAINT PAUL,
MINNESOTA

We thank The David and Lucile Packard Foundation and the
Amherst H. Wilder Foundation for support of this publication.

The Amherst H. Wilder Foundation is one of the largest and oldest endowed human service and community development organizations in the United States. For more than ninety years, the Wilder Foundation has been providing health and human services that help children and families grow strong, the elderly age with dignity, and the community grow in its ability to meet its own needs.

We hope you find this book helpful! Should you need additional information about our services, please contact:

Wilder Center for Communities
Amherst H. Wilder Foundation
919 Lafond Avenue
Saint Paul, MN 55104
Phone 651-642-4022

For more information about other Wilder Foundation publications, please see the back of this book or contact:

Wilder Publishing Center
Amherst H. Wilder Foundation
919 Lafond Avenue
Saint Paul, MN 55104
Phone 800-274-6024
www.wilder.org/pubs

To learn more about LarsonAllen Public Service Group, contact:

LarsonAllen Public Service Group
220 South Sixth Street, Suite 300
Minneapolis, MN 55402-1436
Phone 612-376-4500
www.larsonallen.com/publicservice

Edited by Vincent Hyman and Judith Peacock
Text design by Kirsten Nielsen
Cover design by Rebecca Andrews
Illustrations by Rick Peterson

Manufactured in the United States of America
Second printing, February 2005

Library of Congress Cataloging-in-Publication Data
Ruegg, Debra L.
Bookkeeping basics : what every nonprofit bookkeeper needs to know /
by Debra L. Ruegg and Lisa M. Venkatrathnam.
    p. cm.
Includes bibliographical references and index.
  ISBN 0-940069-29-6 (pbk.)
  1. Nonprofit organizations--Accounting. I. Venkatrathnam, Lisa M.,
1968- II. Title.
HF5686.N56R84 2003
  657'.2--dc21   2002156145

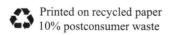
Printed on recycled paper
10% postconsumer waste

Contents

List of Tables

About the Authors

LarsonAllen Public Service Group is one of the leading financial management consulting firms for nonprofits, foundations, and entrepreneurial government entities throughout the United States, specializing in financial and strategic advice, training, and assurance services.

DEBRA L. RUEGG is a principal and senior consultant with the LarsonAllen Public Service Group. Since joining the firm in 1990, she has worked extensively with local and national foundations and nonprofits on financial assessments, financial systems, internal operating systems, and organizational assessments and design. Debra is coauthor of *Budgeting Your Way to Financial Stability.* She is also an experienced and popular trainer in the areas of nonprofit financial management and financial techniques.

LISA M. VENKATRATHNAM is a freelance writer and owner of White Fence Communications. She previously served as a consultant at the LarsonAllen Public Service Group, and has also worked in higher education and church-based initiatives. Lisa is coauthor of *From Spreadsheets to Streetcorners: The 2000 Report on the Financial Health of Minnesota's Nonprofits*; *All the Way to the Bank: Smart Money Management for Tomorrow's Nonprofit*; *Keeping the Books: Developing Financial Capacity in Your Nonprofit Press*, and numerous studies commissioned by foundations and nonprofits across the country.

Acknowledgments

This book would not have been possible without the support and hard work of many individuals. We would like to thank Vince Hyman, Amherst H. Wilder Foundation, for input and advice throughout the writing process; manuscript reviewers William Flowers, Louisa Hackett, Matt Karl, Claire Morduch, Monika Moss, Anita Moreno-Navarro, Gloria Nedved, Jeanne Peters, Liz Schaffer, and Dawn Scranton for their time and input; and most especially the nonprofit practitioners who attended our bookkeeping seminars over the past six years and who helped shape the curriculum that eventually formed the basis of this book.

Preface

In our financial consulting with nonprofits and foundations over the past two decades, we have seen again and again a simple reality: When it comes to nonprofit organizations, one size does not fit all. We have worked with both large and small nonprofits, some with intricate financial systems and others with no systems at all. Regardless of an organization's size, however, financial record keeping is a critical function.

The accounting field is, of course, dedicated to the art and science of financial information. Truth be told, however, many nonprofits don't have a trained bookkeeper on staff, to say nothing of an accountant or financial manager. If this describes your organization, there's good news: With a little bit of education, you can acquire enough knowledge and skills to track the financial activity of your nonprofit in a way that

- Brings order out of chaos
- Safeguards the organization's assets and
- Provides useful information by which to make decisions

This book is intended for nonprofit staff who, whether they have an accounting background or not, are called on to track their organization's financial activity. You might be an executive director, a receptionist, a program manager, or a volunteer board member. Regardless of your position, all we ask is that you are willing to learn. In turn, we'll explain not only how to do things, but also why they're important to do.

You should be forewarned that the world of accounting and bookkeeping has its own rules and vocabulary. A word like "credit" has a specific meaning, and, as much as you may or may not like how the term is used in bookkeeping, you frankly don't have a choice in the matter. Save your creativity for efforts other than bookkeeping and you'll be much happier in the long run. Ironically, as much as bookkeeping is a

This book focuses primarily on manual bookkeeping. Once you have a basic understanding of bookkeeping, you will be in a better position to select a software package that best meets your nonprofit's needs, and you will be able to use that system effectively and accurately.

science, it also requires a certain degree of faith. Some rules won't make much sense at first. Instead of fighting them, accept them at face value knowing you'll eventually see how everything comes together in the end.

One final word of introduction: Computer software programs have made it much easier for groups of all sizes to maintain accurate and up-to-date financial records, without the expense of a full-time bookkeeper or an outside accountant. But like many things in life, accounting software is only as good as the knowledge of the person using it. For this reason, this book focuses primarily on the intricacies of manual bookkeeping. If you don't understand how various pieces of financial information should interrelate on a piece of paper, you won't be able to make it work on a computer system, either. Once you have a basic understanding of bookkeeping, however, you will be in a much better position to select a software package that best meets your nonprofit's needs, and you will be able to use that system effectively and accurately.

Throughout this book you will find examples to illustrate the concepts we discuss in the text. You will also find a detailed glossary of all italicized terms, along with blank sample financial forms. Feel free to copy these forms for your organization to use.

We turn your attention, now, to the basics of bookkeeping and why it is in your organization's best interest to keep good financial records.

Bookkeeping Overview

If you were to list the ten most glamorous jobs in the world, bookkeeping would probably not be among them. But bookkeeping is essential to keep an organization functioning and moving ahead. If it weren't for bookkeeping, organizations wouldn't know how much money they have, how much money they owe, and what money hasn't arrived at the door yet. Bookkeeping provides critical information by which financial decisions are made and plans executed. And the need for good financial decisions is not limited to the for-profit world. Nonprofits, perhaps even more so than their commercial counterparts, need to use their resources wisely. Bookkeeping allows board and management to do just that.

Reality is, however, that many nonprofits don't have a trained bookkeeper on staff, to say nothing of an accountant or financial manager. And so the executive director adds bookkeeping to his or her plate of duties, or a board member offers to help out, or a front-desk receptionist keeps the books in the quieter hours of the week. Many times, these folks have little if any formal accounting training or background. Not only is this frustrating for the individual, but also it is potentially dangerous for the nonprofit. Inaccurate or incomplete bookkeeping opens the door for poor financial decisions, misuse of funds, and, in extreme cases, fraud.

We say this not to alarm you (well, perhaps just a bit!) but rather to indicate that we understand where you are, where you need to be, and how you can get there. Even if you've never opened a bookkeeping textbook in your life, you're in luck! This book will help you to successfully meet the basic bookkeeping requirements of your organization.

Bookkeeping Defined

So what exactly is bookkeeping? In a nutshell, *bookkeeping** is the recording of financial transactions so their effect can be shown in financial statements. Bookkeeping documents money that flows into, out of, and throughout an organization, organizes this information in a consistent and uniform way, and summarizes the data so that a bigger financial picture emerges.

Bookkeeping versus accounting

While some people refer to "bookkeeping" and "accounting" interchangeably, these terms actually represent distinct activities. Bookkeeping's primary focus is to record financial activity. *Accounting* includes bookkeeping but goes beyond it in scope. Accounting also involves activities such as designing financial systems, establishing controls to make sure these systems work well, and analyzing and verifying financial information produced by these systems. Simply put, bookkeeping is the record-keeping aspect of accounting.

The Importance of Good Financial Records

The financial records produced by a good bookkeeping system are critical in several ways. Financial records help board and management make well-informed decisions. They keep the organization running smoothly. And, they help your nonprofit maintain financial accountability to the outside world.

Advantages of Good Financial Records

- Financial information helps board and management make well-informed decisions.
- Financial records keep the organization running smoothly.
- Financial records help your nonprofit maintain financial accountability to the outside world.

Help board and management make well-informed decisions

Financial records facilitate the preparation of reports showing the financial condition of your nonprofit. These reports allow your organization's board and management to determine how much it costs to provide a certain service or activity, project future funding needs, and assess the overall financial health of the organization. Without accurate financial records, informed decisions simply cannot be made.

Keep the organization running smoothly

A good bookkeeping system is essential to keep an organization on track financially. Imagine, for instance, an organization that is not able to easily identify what bills it owes, how much money remains to be spent from a particular grant, or if there is enough income to meet this month's expenses. Good financial records bring order out of chaos and save time and energy in the long run. Just ask anyone who has had to "re-create" last year's financial information with only a shocbox of receipts in hand!

---

* Words that appear in italics are included in the glossary.

Demonstrate financial accountability to the outside world

If the first two reasons for maintaining a good bookkeeping system are not compelling enough, this last one usually is. As your nonprofit increases in size and complexity, so, too, will the need to report to outside funders, the government, and other constituents. Not only will board and management need to report on the financial condition of your organization, they will also need to provide assurance that sufficient internal controls are in place to safeguard your organization's assets. A good financial record-keeping system allows you to do just that.

The Three Steps of Bookkeeping

All bookkeeping activities fall into one of three categories: documenting, recording, and summarizing. Here's a broad overview of each of these functions.

1. Documenting

The first step in bookkeeping is to collect evidence of (or document) financial transactions. When any financial transaction takes place, some sort of paper or receipt should show the amount of money, the date, and the people involved in the transaction. Such papers or receipts are called *source documents,* and they are the raw data from which financial records start. Examples of source documents include checks, deposit receipts, and invoices for money the organization owes (known as *accounts payable*) and for money that someone owes the organization (known as *accounts receivable*).

Chapter Four will look more closely at the documenting process.

THE 3 STEPS OF Bookkeeping

1. DOCUMENTING   2. RECORDING   3. SUMMARIZING

2. Recording

Once your source documents are collected, you will need to list the transactions in chronological order. This process is called *recording* or journalizing. Any book that contains a chronological list of transactions is called a *journal.*

The most familiar form of a journal is the checkbook. It gives a record of each transaction and a running balance in the account. Checkbooks, however, are limited in the information they can provide. For instance, a checkbook balance does not reflect what your organization owes or what others owe to your organization. (As discussed in Chapter Two, this limitation is a significant difference between *cash basis* and *accrual basis* accounting.)

Chapter Four also takes a closer look at recording and posting transactions and the various journals, ledgers, and accounts you will use in your bookkeeping role.

3. Summarizing

Ultimately, the bookkeeping system must break down all financial information into categories that will be shown on financial statements. For instance, what financial transactions impacted the organization's income and expenses? What financial transactions impacted the organization's *assets* (what you own) and *liabilities* (what you owe)?

By accumulating the effects of all transactions on each financial category, the bookkeeping system produces the figures needed for financial statements. The most common financial statements produced for nonprofits are the statement of position (also known as the balance sheet) and the statement of activities (also known as the income statement). The *statement of position* provides a financial snapshot of your organization at a particular point in time—what your organization owns, what it owes, and the difference between these two amounts—in other words, your organization's net worth. The *statement of activities* shows where your income came from, where it was spent, and how much you had left (*surplus*) or were short (*deficit*) over the course of a certain period.

Chapters Five and Six will look more closely at these financial statements and how they are created.

The three primary activities of bookkeeping—documenting, recording, and summarizing financial transactions—create the information needed by every nonprofit to make good financial decisions and plan for the future. We now turn your attention to the conceptual framework behind basic accounting methods.

Chapter One Key Concepts

- Bookkeeping is the recording of financial transactions so their effect can be shown in financial statements. While some people refer to bookkeeping and accounting interchangeably, these terms are actually distinct. Bookkeeping is the record-keeping aspect of accounting. All bookkeeping activities fall into one of three categories: documenting, recording, and summarizing.

- Good financial records are critical to nonprofits in several ways. Financial records help board and management make well-informed decisions, keep the organization running smoothly, and help the nonprofit maintain financial accountability to the outside world.

Setting the Stage

Before getting started in the bookkeeping process, we're going to examine the conceptual framework behind basic accounting methods. If you're one of those practical-minded folks who want to get to the "how-to" of this book, you may be tempted to rush through this chapter. Don't. The concepts in this chapter are critical to setting the stage for the practical tasks and procedures you'll undertake soon enough.

You may be tempted to rush through this chapter. Don't. The concepts in this chapter are critical to setting the stage for the practical tasks and procedures you'll undertake soon enough.

Cash Basis Versus Accrual Basis Accounting

One of the earliest financial decisions that your organization must make is whether to use the cash basis or accrual basis method of accounting. This decision relates to the timing of the recording and reporting of *income* and *expenses*.

Some financial transactions involve the immediate transfer of cash. Suppose, however, an organization buys office supplies on credit. It receives the supplies in exchange for a promise to pay cash in the future. In accounting terms, the organization has an *account payable,* that is, an obligation to pay. Likewise, an organization may perform a service and then issue a bill for the service. The person billed has an obligation to pay the bill, but the money won't reach the organization until some time later. In accounting terms, the organization has an *account receivable,* that is, an expectation of receiving payment.

The cash versus accrual question arises when an organization decides at what point to recognize income and expenses on the books. *Cash basis accounting* records income only when cash is received, and records expenses at the time they are actually paid, similar to entries in a checkbook. This is the simpler way to keep financial records, but it fails to reflect the actual financial condition of the organization. For instance, your organization would not be able to tell if income has been earned but not yet received, or if expenses have been incurred but not yet paid. Without knowing these critical pieces of information, planning becomes difficult because you do not have your organization's complete financial picture.

Accrual basis accounting, on the other hand, records income when it is earned and expenses when they are incurred. This represents the true financial condition of the organization because it records all income and expenses, whether paid or not. The accrual basis method takes into account whether or not the organization has inventory, payroll expenses (especially withholdings and taxes), grants designated for specific purposes, and other specific financial activity that is not reflected in cash transactions.

If your organization is required to have its financial statements audited by a *certified public accountant (CPA),* your year-end financial records must conform with *generally accepted accounting principles (GAAP)*—and that means accounting on the accrual basis. Smaller organizations, however, may maintain their internal financial records either on a cash or an accrual basis.

For smaller organizations, the ideal method depends on the nature of their income and expenses. If an organization typically has outstanding income (such as designated grants) or outstanding expenses (such as large payroll withholdings) that significantly impact its financial position, then the accrual method should be used. If, on the other hand, outstanding income and expenses do not noticeably affect the organization's financial position, a cash basis method is appropriate and simpler to use. A conversation with an auditor or a CPA may clarify which method should be used.

If your organization uses the cash basis method of accounting, we still encourage you to think with an accrual mentality. Keep your eye on the timing and cycles of expenses and income—keep a record of unpaid bills and earned income not yet received—and your organization will be able to make more informed decisions as a result.

Double-Entry Bookkeeping

There are two basic methods of bookkeeping: single-entry bookkeeping and double-entry bookkeeping. The *single-entry* method utilizes only income and expense accounts, similar to what many individuals use in recording their personal finances in a checkbook. Transactions are recorded only once. *Double-entry bookkeeping* uses a wider

---

**Example:
Cash Basis Versus Accrual Basis Entries**

Your organization submits a bill of $3,000 to the local county on April 3 for services performed in March. You receive payment from the county on April 30.

Cash Basis: On April 3, no record-keeping entry is required because no cash has been exchanged between your organization and the county. You wouldn't record an entry until April 30, at which time you would recognize $3,000 in cash received and revenue earned. Under this scenario, the organization's March financial statements will give no indication that services had been performed for which payment is expected.

Accrual Basis: On March 31, you would recognize $3,000 in revenue (March 31 being the last day of the month in which services were performed). You would also record that the organization has an account receivable of $3,000, meaning that your organization has earned money but not yet received it. When the money is received from the county on April 30, you would make additional entries to indicate that payment had been received and the bill is no longer outstanding. Under this scenario, the organization's March financial statements will show that services have been performed for which payment is expected. April financial statements will show that payment has been received.

variety of accounts and records every transaction twice. Our focus in this book is on the double-entry method. As we will show in the following section, this method provides a critical safeguard for your organization's assets. It is also the required method for organizations of any size and complexity.

In double-entry bookkeeping, every financial transaction has two sides. Every transaction must be recorded in at least two accounts—as a debit entry in one account and as a credit entry in another. At this point, erase from your mind whatever ideas you may have about the meaning of the terms "debit" and "credit." One does not mean "negative" and the other "positive," nor does one mean "decrease" and the other "increase." For bookkeeping purposes, *debit* means the left side of the ledger page and *credit* means the right side of the ledger page. That's all, no more and no less. (Here's an instance of needing to take a rule at face value and not read deeper meaning into it.) Remember, debit = left, credit = right.

The financial statements of your organization have several major categories, such as assets, liabilities, net assets, contributions, earned revenue, and operating expenses. Within these major categories are numerous subcategories called *accounts*. Together, all of these accounts make up the *general ledger*. Every financial transaction affects at least two accounts and each account has two sides to keep track of resources coming in and going out.

Pop quiz: What's the left side of the ledger called? You've got it! Left = debit, right = credit. Bonus point: How many times should every financial transaction be recorded? That's right, at least twice—as a debit entry in one account and as a credit entry in another.

Now that you have these two basic rules down, we'll add a layer of complexity. For all asset and expense accounts, a debit entry (left side) indicates an increase in the account balance and a credit entry (right side) indicates a decrease. Conversely, for all liability, net asset, and income accounts, a credit entry (right side) indicates an increase in the account balance and a debit entry (left side) indicates a decrease. This may not make much sense at first, but give it time and you'll see how it all fits together. (Also see the sidebar on page 12.)

One advantage of the double-entry system is the ease of determining the current balance of each account and exactly how much money has gone into and out of each account in a given period. To do this manually, simply total the debits and credits in each account. A computerized system will indicate the balance automatically. An account with more debits than credits is said to have a *debit balance*. An account with more credits than debits is said to have a *credit balance*. Remember, a debit balance does not necessarily mean that the account has a shortage or deficit. Rather, it simply means that the sum of dollars on the left side of the account is greater than the total of the right side.

TIP!

Know how double-entry bookkeeping works

It is important to understand how the double-entry system works, even if your accounting software makes debit and credit entries for you. Not only is the double-entry system required for organizations of any size and complexity, but also, once you understand this system, it will be much easier to find errors if the accounts fail to balance.

As we will discuss in Chapter Five, your organization should produce at least two financial reports on a monthly basis: a statement of position and a statement of activities. These two reports summarize the bookkeeping process. Organizations will have some accounts with a debit balance and some with a credit balance. For financially healthy organizations, normal statement of position account balances are as follows:

- *Asset accounts* (what the organization owns, such as cash, inventory, and accounts receivable) normally have debit balances, meaning the total of the left side is greater than the total of the right side.

- *Liability accounts* (what the organization owes, such as accounts payable, loans, and accrued salaries) normally have credit balances, meaning the total of the right side of the account is greater than the total of the left side.

- *Net asset accounts* (the difference between an organization's total assets and total liabilities) will normally have a credit balance, meaning the total of the right side of the account is greater than the total of the left side.

Table 1 summarizes assets, liabilities, and net assets.

TABLE 1. Summary of Debit and Credit Entries on Statement of Position Accounts (Assets, Liabilities, and Net Assets)

	Sample Accounts	Effect of Debit and Credit Entries	Normal Account Balance
Statement of Position			
Assets (what your organization owns)	Cash Inventory Accounts receivable	A debit entry will increase an asset account balance; a credit entry will decrease the account balance	Debit balance
Liabilities (what your organization owes)	Accounts payable Loans Accrued salaries	A credit entry will increase a liability account balance; a debit entry will decrease the account balance	Credit balance
Net Assets (the difference between your organization's total assets and total liabilities; also called "net worth")	Unrestricted net assets Temporarily restricted net assets Permanently restricted net assets	Entries to the net asset accounts are made only at year-end through closing entries or audit adjustments	A credit balance indicates a surplus or positive net worth; a debit balance indicates negative net worth

For financially healthy organizations, normal statement of activities account balances are as follows:

- *Income accounts* (money flowing into the organization, such as foundation grants, individual contributions, earned revenue, and interest revenue) normally have credit balances and, in fact, usually reflect only credit transactions, unless your organization is making a refund to someone. (When you refund money already paid to you, you would debit the income account.)

- *Expense accounts* (money paid by the organization, such as salaries, office supplies, postage and shipping, and occupancy charges) typically have debit balances and usually reflect only debit transactions, unless someone is making a refund to your organization.

Table 2 summarizes income and expense accounts.

The overarching rule of double-entry bookkeeping is this: *When all is said and done, the total of all debits must equal the total of all credits.*

TABLE 2. Summary of Debit and Credit Entries on Statement of Activities Accounts (Income and Expenses)

	Sample Accounts	Effect of Debit and Credit Entries	Normal Account Balance
Statement of Activities			
Income (money flowing into your organization)	Foundation grants Individual contributions Earned revenue Interest revenue	A credit entry will increase an income account balance; a debit entry will decrease the account balance	Credit balance
Expenses (money paid by your organization)	Salaries Office supplies Postage and shipping Occupancy charges	A debit entry will increase an expense account balance; a credit entry will decrease the account balance	Debit balance

---

As we shall see later in this book, every transaction you *post* (record) to your accounts adds up to create the financial picture of your organization. The overarching rule of double-entry bookkeeping is this: *When all is said and done, the total of all debits must equal the total of all credits.* If they don't, you know that an entry was missed or inaccurately recorded somewhere along the way. By requiring total debits and total credits to be equal, the double-entry system serves as a critical safeguard for your organization's assets.

Effect of Debit and Credit Entries on Various Types of Accounts

	Debit	Credit	Normal Balance
Assets	↑	↓	Debit
Liabilities	↓	↑	Credit
Net Assets	↓	↑	Credit
Income	↓	↑	Credit
Expense	↑	↓	Debit

To review, the double-entry system of bookkeeping is based on the following set of rules:

- Every financial transaction has two sides.
- For every transaction, at least one account is debited and one account is credited.
- Debit refers to the left side of the ledger page and credit refers to the right side of the ledger page.
- For all asset and expense accounts, a debit entry indicates an increase in the account balance and a credit entry indicates a decrease. Conversely, for all liability, net asset, and income accounts, a credit entry indicates an increase in the account balance and a debit entry indicates a decrease.
- Asset and expense accounts normally have debit balances, while liability, net asset, and income accounts normally have credit balances.
- The total of all debits must equal the total of all credits.

By recording both sides of a transaction using the double-entry system, you ensure that your financial assets are safeguarded. The double-entry system also allows you to easily determine the current balance of each account and exactly how much money has gone into and out of each account in a given period.

Now that we've presented the conceptual framework behind double-entry bookkeeping, we'll discuss your organization's accounts in more detail and recommend ways to organize them most effectively.

Chapter Two Key Concepts

- While cash basis accounting is the simpler way to keep financial records, accrual basis accounting—recognizing income when it is earned and expenses when they are incurred—better represents the true financial condition of the organization.
- Double-entry bookkeeping provides a safeguard for your organization's financial assets. For every transaction, at least one account is debited and one account is credited. To balance, the total of all debits must equal the total of all credits.

Your Chart of Accounts

To facilitate the tracking of your organization's financial transactions, you will need to develop a comprehensive listing of the accounts you use and plan to use. This listing, called a *chart of accounts,* identifies each account with a name and a number.

A chart of accounts allows you to group similar transactions and show their cumulative effect on your organization's financial position. For example, by grouping all contributions together, you can report the total amount contributed to your organization over a certain period. By grouping all salaries together, you can report total salary expense separate from office supplies or occupancy expenses.

A chart of accounts can be used in several ways. It can highlight the activities of your organization, categorize income and expense activities, segregate different types of assets, liabilities, and net assets, and facilitate preparation of your agency's financial statements and external reports.

When you sit down to design a chart of accounts, remember that careful planning at the beginning will save you time in the long run. Proceed systematically by thinking carefully about what your organization does and who needs to know about it. Too much detail is better than not enough; it is always easier to summarize existing data into broader categories than to report on detail that wasn't recorded in the first place.

You should consider many factors when creating your chart of accounts. What do managers, staff, and board members need to know? What does the public need to know? What are the reporting requirements of the Internal Revenue Service (IRS) or specific funders? What format best meets the needs of internal decision makers? What format is required

TIP!

Your chart of accounts should be flexible to meet a variety of needs

When designing your chart of accounts, keep in mind who will need what type of information and in what format. It is always easier to summarize existing data into broader categories than to report on detail that wasn't recorded in the first place.

by external constituents? All of these factors will help determine the scope and complexity of your chart of accounts. Remember, this is a tool to ultimately help you be more effective in your job, so design it with the end products in mind. The steps that follow will help you design your chart of accounts.

Designing Your Chart of Accounts

There are five basic steps to setting up a chart of accounts:

1. Define your programs and cost centers.
2. Identify specific line items.
3. Highlight funding sources that require detailed financial reports.
4. Segregate unrestricted, temporarily restricted, and permanently restricted funds.
5. Number your accounts.

1. Define your programs and cost centers

The first step to creating your chart of accounts is to think about the big picture of your organization: What are its core programs and *cost centers?* To illustrate, we have listed in the sample below the core programs and cost centers of a fictitious nonprofit called Horizon Arts Organization. Horizon Arts operates three mission-specific programs—an arts discovery class, an arts education class, and a community arts gallery. Horizon Arts lists "administration" and "fundraising" as cost centers, in addition to its mission-specific programs. Since the IRS requires nonprofits to report on administration (sometimes referred to as "management and general") and fundraising as distinct categories, you should also include these in your list of program services and cost centers. In addition, if your organization hosts an annual event or conference, you may set this event up as a separate cost center to track its expenses.

Sample Programs and Cost Centers for Horizon Arts Organization

Arts discovery class

Arts education collaborative with local school districts

Community arts gallery

Administration

Fundraising

---

2. Identify specific line items

The next step to creating your chart of accounts is to identify specific line items on which you need to report. Tables 3 and 4 on page 16 list line items most commonly used by nonprofit organizations, such as salaries, supplies, occupancy, foundation grants, and individual contributions.

A couple of things to note about line items: First, line items fall into one of two overarching categories: statement of position accounts and statement of activities accounts. Second, they are further organized into the five major categories we talked about earlier: assets, liabilities, net assets, income, and expenses.

Normal accounting practice dictates that statement of position items be listed in order of *liquidity* (how easily or quickly an item can be converted to cash), with the most liquid items listed first (such as checking accounts or investments), followed by less liquid or "non-current" items (such as inventory or buildings). Statement of activities items are typically listed in order of size, with the largest sources of income and largest expenses listed first. This order will also be reflected on your actual financial statements.

TIP!

How to choose the right accounting software

When researching accounting software programs, consider features such as system adaptability (flexibility of the chart of accounts, modules available, and integration between modules), reporting flexibility, hardware requirements, ease of use, and availability of technical support. An effective computerized accounting system should have a three-part chart-of-accounts structure that allows your organization to track and report information by program/cost center, line item detail, and funding source. It should also have the capability to segregate temporarily and permanently restricted net assets.

Some of the specific line items in Tables 3 and 4, page 16, may be new to you. While we will discuss these terms later in the text, you can refer to the glossary for immediate reference. You may also notice that some of the sample line items, such as "allowance for doubtful accounts" and "accumulated depreciation," are shown in parentheses. In the accounting world, parentheses are often used to indicate that a figure is a negative amount or should be subtracted from the total amount. Very rarely will you see a negative or minus sign used for negative amounts.

Allowance for doubtful accounts and accumulated depreciation represent contra-asset accounts. A *contra-asset account* reduces the value of a specific asset account. For example, assets such as equipment are purchased with the intent that they will benefit the organization for a number of years. However, these assets become less valuable as time passes. Financial record-keeping rules specify that financial statements reflect the true value of what the organization owns through the recording of accumulated depreciation.

The same method is used when presenting the correct value of accounts receivable (money someone owes your organization). Accounts receivable may become less collectable after time passes. The organization may record an allowance for doubtful accounts to accurately reflect the amount of accounts receivable the organization believes it will be able to collect.

We will further discuss accumulated depreciation and allowance for doubtful accounts in Chapter Eight.

TABLE 3. Sample Line Items for a Statement of Position

Assets

Current assets
  Cash – checking
  Cash – savings
  Investments
  Petty cash
  Accounts receivable
  (Allowance for doubtful accounts)
  Grants and contributions receivable
  Prepaid expenses
  Security deposits

Fixed assets
  Furniture and fixtures
  Equipment
  Software
  Leasehold improvements
  (Accumulated depreciation)
  (Accumulated amortization)

Other assets

Liabilities

Current liabilities
  Accounts payable
  Loans/notes payable – current portion
  Current maturities – long-term debt
  Accrued salaries payable
  Medicare withholding
  Social Security withholding
  Federal withholding
  State withholding
  Retirement fund payable
  Other accrued payroll taxes
  Accrued vacation
  Deferred revenue

Long-term liabilities
  Loans/notes payable
  Capital lease payable

Net Assets

Unrestricted net assets
Temporarily restricted net assets
Permanently restricted net assets
Current year surplus/(deficit)

TABLE 4. Sample Line Items for a Statement of Activities

Income

Support
  Foundation grants
  Corporate grants
  Government grants
  Individual contributions
  In-kind contributions
  Net assets released from restriction

Earned revenue
  Contracts
  Interest/investment revenue
  Fees
  Special event revenue
  Other revenue

Expenses

Personnel costs
  Salaries
  Payroll taxes
  Employee benefits

General expenses
  Professional fees
  Supplies
  Telephone
  Postage and shipping
  Occupancy
  Equipment rental and maintenance
  Insurance
  Travel
  Employee training
  Interest expense
  Dues and subscriptions
  Bank charges
  Miscellaneous
  Depreciation
  Amortization

3. Highlight funding sources that require detailed financial reports

The third step to creating your chart of accounts is to identify funding sources that require detailed financial reports, such as *grants* and government contracts. Some funding sources only want assurance that you have spent the funds on a specific program. In that case, you may only need to track revenue separately. In other cases, funders require their grants or contracts be spent on specific categories of expenses or expenses such as salaries or rent. For these funders, you will need to track more detail. If your accounting software does not allow for additional segregation, you can track this information on spreadsheet software.

To illustrate the third step, we have listed below the grants and contracts for which Horizon Arts Organization will need to develop separate funding reports. Notice we have included both types of income Horizon Arts Organization uses to fund its activities, *earned* (VA School District #920 contract and State of Virginia contract) and *contributed* (Highview Foundation grant and National Endowment for the Arts grant).

In addition to funding sources, you should identify other groups to whom your organization must report financial information, including the IRS. What type of information will you need to report? As mentioned earlier, the IRS will require you to distinguish between program, administrative, and fundraising activities.

The distinguishing feature among unrestricted, temporarily restricted, and permanently restricted net assets is the donor's intent.

Sample Funding Sources Requiring Separate Reports for Horizon Arts Organization

VA School District #920 contract

State of Virginia contract

Highview Foundation grant

National Endowment for the Arts (NEA) grant

---

4. Segregate unrestricted, temporarily restricted, and permanently restricted funds

Donations are a critical source of income for most nonprofits. Because of this, nonprofits are required to track their funds according to three specific categories: unrestricted, temporarily restricted, and permanently restricted funds. We will delve into this topic in greater detail in Chapter Six. As a quick overview, the distinguishing feature among these categories is the donor's intent. *Unrestricted net assets* do not have any donor restrictions imposed on them and are therefore available for general use by the nonprofit. *Temporarily restricted net assets* are contributions received by a nonprofit with donor restrictions that will eventually expire or will be fulfilled by an action of the organization. *Permanently restricted net assets* are those contributed resources on which the donor has placed a restriction that will never expire. Net assets are considered restricted only if the donor restricts their use. All other assets, including board-designated amounts, are legally considered unrestricted.

For purposes here, suffice it to say that your chart of accounts will need to indicate whether funds are unrestricted, temporarily restricted, or permanently restricted. As you begin to classify your funds, we encourage you to read Chapter Six in detail. Depending on the complexity of your funding sources, you may also need to consult with your auditor or a CPA to make sure you are tracking your funds in accordance with legal classifications.

Sample Temporarily Restricted Funds for Horizon Arts Organization

Horizon Arts Organization has two grants that are considered temporarily restricted:

1. Highview Foundation grant: Horizon Arts must complete one semester of arts education classes in six elementary schools before requirements of the first half of the grant are met; after completion of a second semester of classes, the full terms of the grant will have been met and funds will no longer be considered temporarily restricted.

2. NEA grant: Horizon Arts received a two-year grant from the National Endowment for the Arts (NEA) to conduct arts discovery classes throughout the state. Restrictions will expire with the passage of time.

At this time, Horizon Arts does not have any permanently restricted funds. All other funds are considered unrestricted.

---

5. Number your accounts

The final step in designing your chart of accounts is to number your accounts. To do this, you will need to number your programs and cost centers, funding sources that require separate or unique reports, and line item details.

For your programs/cost centers and funding sources, we recommend using at least a two-digit numbering system, as illustrated in the example below of Horizon Arts. Funding sources that do *not* require separate reports (such as earned income sources) do not need a numeric code. If a number is required by your bookkeeping software, you may choose to default to "00" for these items.

Sample Numbering Accounts: Horizon Arts Programs and Funders

Programs and cost centers		Funding sources	
Administration	01	VA School District #920 contract	01
Fundraising	02	State of Virginia contract	02
Arts discovery class	03	Highview Foundation grant	03
Arts education collaborative	04	NEA grant	04
Community arts gallery	05		

You will next need to number your line items. For ease of use, assign the same number range for all accounts of one type, as shown in Table 5. So, for instance, all assets will be in the 1000 range, all liabilities will be in the 2000 range, and so forth. Because of the potential for a large number of line items, we recommend using a four-digit numbering system for your line items. The range of numbers for each account category will facilitate adding new accounts in future years.

TABLE 5. Sample Ranges for Line Item Numbering

Statement of Position Accounts		Statement of Activities Accounts	
Assets: 1010-1999		Income: 4010-5999	
Current assets	1010-1499	Support	4010-4999
Fixed assets	1500-1799	Earned revenue	5010-5999
Other assets	1800-1999	Expenses: 6010-7999	
Liabilities: 2010-2999		Personnel costs	6010-6999
Current liabilities	2010-2499	General expenses	7010-7999
Long-term liabilities	2500-2999		
Net assets: 3010-3999			
Unrestricted net assets	3010-3199		
Temporarily restricted net assets	3200-3299		
Permanently restricted net assets	3300-3399		
Current year surplus/(deficit)	3510		

Tables 6 and 7, page 20, are sample line item charts of accounts for statement of position accounts and statement of activities accounts. Line items listed in the chart of accounts without an account number represent subtotals and totals computed on the actual financial statements. Too much detail in a financial statement, especially one presented to the board or outside readers, can cause confusion and detract from the reader's understanding of the overall financial picture.

Once your numbering system is in place, you will be able to code your organization's financial transactions by program/cost center, funding source, and line item. If you use computerized accounting software, your software will determine the format of your chart of accounts. For purposes of illustration, Horizon Arts' chart of accounts is formatted as follows:

Program/Cost Center	Funding Source	Line Item
XX	XX	XXXX

TABLE 6. Sample Line Item Chart of Accounts for a Statement of Position

Account #	Account Description
Assets	

Current assets

1010	Cash – checking
1020	Cash – savings
1030	Investments
1040	Petty cash
1210	Accounts receivable
1220	(Allowance for doubtful accounts)
1310	Grants and contributions receivable
1410	Prepaid expenses
1420	Security deposits

Fixed assets

1710	Furniture and fixtures
1720	Equipment
1730	Software
1740	Leasehold improvements
1750	(Accumulated depreciation)
1760	(Accumulated amortization)

Other assets

1810	Other assets

Liabilities

Current liabilities

2010	Accounts payable
2110	Loans/notes payable – current portion
2120	Current maturities – long-term debt
2210	Accrued salaries payable
2220	Medicare withholding
2221	Social Security withholding
2230	Federal withholding
2240	State withholding
2250	Retirement fund payable
2260	Other accrued payroll taxes
2270	Accrued vacation
2410	Deferred revenue

Long-term liabilities

2510	Loans/notes payable
2520	Capital lease payable

Net Assets

3110	Unrestricted net assets
3210	Temporarily restricted net assets
3310	Permanently restricted net assets
3510	Current year surplus/(deficit)

TABLE 7. Sample Line Item Chart of Accounts for a Statement of Activities

Account #	Account Description
Income	

Support

4010	Foundation grants
4020	Corporate grants
4030	Government grants
4110	Individual contributions
4210	In-kind contributions
4300	Net assets released from restriction

Earned revenue

5010	Contracts
5020	Interest/investment revenue
5100	Fees
5110	Special event revenue
5210	Other revenue

Expenses

Personnel costs

6010	Salaries
6020	Payroll taxes
6030	Employee benefits

General expenses

7010	Professional fees
7110	Supplies
7120	Telephone
7130	Postage and shipping
7140	Occupancy
7150	Equipment rental and maintenance
7160	Insurance
7170	Travel
7210	Employee training
7310	Interest expense
7410	Dues and subscriptions
7420	Bank charges
7430	Miscellaneous
7510	Depreciation
7520	Amortization

We'll say that Horizon Arts Organization incurs $3,500 in salary expenses for an employee working in the arts discovery class program, funded by the Highview Foundation grant. Based on Horizon Arts' chart of accounts, that expense would be numbered as follows:

```
03-03-6010
```

The first "03" represents the program/cost center (arts discovery class), the middle "03" represents the funding source (Highview Foundation grant), and "6010" represents the line item (salaries).

Depending on your bookkeeping system, a third digit could be added either to the program/cost center code or to the funding source code to designate whether a fund is unrestricted, temporarily restricted, or permanently restricted. The general format would look something like this:

```
XX1 = unrestricted
XX2 = temporarily restricted
XX3 = permanently restricted
```

In Horizon Arts' instance, we added a third digit to its funding source code to designate whether a fund was unrestricted (XX1), temporarily restricted (XX2), or permanently restricted (XX3). So, for example, when a contract was signed with the local school district to complete arts education classes, the transaction was coded as follows:

```
04-011-5010
```

The "04" represents the program/cost center (arts education collaborative), the "011" represents the funding source and net asset restriction (VA School District #920, unrestricted), and the "5010" represents the specific line item (contracts). (As we will discuss in Chapter Six, the VA school district contract represents earned revenue and therefore is considered unrestricted.)

This type of coding system provides the framework you need to prepare your organization's statement of position and statement of activities. It also allows you to prepare a wide variety of other reports to help your organization evaluate its activities and report to outside constituents and funders. Based on Horizon Arts' chart of accounts, for instance, you could determine

- How much money has been received in foundation grants year-to-date
- How much the organization has spent from a particular grant, and how much of the grant remains

TIP!

Determine how to allocate indirect expenses

Some expenses are not direct program expenses but benefit the organization as a whole. These expenses are charged against the administrative cost center. You will need to determine a method for allocating these costs (sometimes referred to as "overhead" or "indirect costs") so that each program bears an appropriate share. Organizations approach this allocation in a variety of ways. For instance, expenses can be charged back to programs on the basis of the percent of square footage that they occupy. Others allocate indirect expenses based on the percentage that each program represents in the budget, or on the basis of the percentage of staff time spent in each program. Whatever method you choose, the important point is that you use it consistently.

- How much the organization spent in occupancy-related expenses last year
- How much the organization currently owes in payroll taxes
- How much it costs to operate a program
- How much the organization has in unrestricted funds

These are just a few examples of how a chart of accounts can be used. The time you spend in planning your chart of accounts is well worth it! A carefully structured chart of accounts can effectively serve your organization for many years to come. In the next chapter, we'll show how to record transactions.

Chapter Three Key Concepts

- The building block for your bookkeeping system is the chart of accounts. When you sit down to design a chart of accounts, remember that careful planning at the beginning will save you time in the long run. Proceed systematically by thinking carefully about what your organization does and who needs to know about it. Too much detail is better than not enough.

- There are five basic steps to setting up a chart of accounts: (1) define your programs and cost centers; (2) identify specific line items; (3) highlight funding sources that require detailed financial reports; (4) segregate unrestricted, temporarily restricted, and permanently restricted funds; (5) and number your accounts.

Recording Transactions

Now that you have set up your chart of accounts, you are ready to begin recording financial transactions. This chapter looks at several key activities in the recording process: documenting transactions, making journal entries, posting transactions to the general ledger, and preparing a trial balance.

Source Documents

The bookkeeping process begins when you collect *source documents* such as bills, invoices, receipts, checks, deposit slips, and bank statements. Generally speaking, source documents (also known as an "audit trail" or "paper trail") should be kept on file for a minimum of three years. Cancelled checks can be discarded after this time, but make sure to keep a file of all corresponding bank statements.

Since source documents form the basis of your historical record, make sure to organize them with some sort of logical consistency. If you can't find your source documents at a later time, it won't matter that you saved them. We find it helpful to organize documents by several categories: payroll, income source, vendors, source documents, bank records, audit file and tax records, and fixed assets. See Table 8, page 24, for a summary of information to include in each of these files. Refer to Chapters Eight and Nine for suggested ways to organize your records.

ALWAYS KEEP A PAPER TRAIL!

Journal Entries

Once your source documents are collected, it is time to record the information in a journal. A *journal* (also referred to as a *register*) is simply a chronological list of financial transactions. A journal allows you to reference basic information about a transaction, including when it happened and what accounts were debited and credited (remember that in double-entry bookkeeping, every financial transaction impacts at least two accounts).

You should make journal entries on a regular basis. For organizations with a high volume of transactions, entries should be made daily. For smaller organizations, weekly or even biweekly will be sufficient.

A *journal entry* should include several basic pieces of information:

- Date of transaction
- Source document number if available (Example: invoice number)
- Description
- Account(s) to be debited, and by how much
- Account(s) to be credited, and by how much

When you record a journal entry, note on the source document what account was debited and what account was credited. This will serve as a handy reference if you need to check the transaction later.

TABLE 8. Internal Documentation and Filing Systems

Payroll files

- Maintain basic information on all employees including Social Security numbers and dates of employment
- Maintain copies of all IRS W-4 forms (completed and signed by employees to determine income tax withholdings)
- Maintain documentation related to all wage and salary actions
- Maintain copies of quarterly and annual payroll tax filings (both federal and state)

Income source files

- Maintain copies of checks received with related correspondence

Vendor files

- Maintain copies of vendor invoices, bills, and payments by fiscal period (month, quarter, or fiscal year)

Source document files

- Maintain copies of receipts, bills, and other general source documents by fiscal period (month, quarter, or fiscal year)

Bank records

- Maintain bank statements and other bank records both by fiscal period and by bank account
- File completed bank reconciliation forms with corresponding bank statements

Audit file and tax records

- Maintain tax records by fiscal year
- Maintain copies of all audit-related working papers (see Table 21, Audit Preparation Checklist, page 54)

Fixed asset files

- Maintain chronological listing of all fixed asset purchases, including description, date purchased, cost, and method used to calculate depreciation

As you will quickly see, the more familiar you become with how to debit and credit accounts, the easier it will be to make journal entries. For a quick review of double-entry bookkeeping, see the sidebar Double-Entry Bookkeeping in Review on page 26.

To illustrate the process of making journal entries, we'll use Northwest Housing Alliance, a fictitious nonprofit organization, as an example. On January 14, the following transactions need to be made:

1. Receive the January electric bill for $250 and enter into accounts payable. Payment is due by January 31.

2. Pay the December telephone bill of $75, due January 20.

3. Pay $550 monthly installment on the organization's cash-flow loan with $500 principal and $50 interest expense.

4. Receive a letter from Central Community Foundation confirming grant award of $5,000 and enter in grants receivable.

5. Receive semimonthly payroll detail from payroll service of $2,200 gross payroll. Includes $2,000 salaries and $200 employer payroll taxes.

> **TIP!**
>
> **Always keep a paper trail!**
>
> When bookkeeping systems are computerized, it can be especially tempting to become lazy and not maintain proper documentation. Don't fall into this habit. We guarantee that your life will become miserable when you are asked to prove where your numbers came from! Always keep source documents on file for a minimum of three years.

These transactions would be entered onto a journal page as shown in Table 9.

TABLE 9. Northwest Housing Alliance—Sample Journal Page

Date	Description of Entry	Account Name and Number		Document Number	Debit	Credit
1/14/02	January electric	Occupancy expense	7140	1/15/02 Elec	$250	
		Accounts payable	2010			$250
1/14/02	December telephone	Accounts payable	2010	12/31/02 Tele	$75	
		Cash	1010			$75
1/14/02	January loan	Loans and notes payable	2110	January-02	$500	
		Interest expense	7310		$50	
		Cash	1010			$550
1/14/02	Central Community Foundation	Grants and contributions receivable	1310	Grant reference #1032	$5,000	
		Foundation grants	4010			$5,000
1/14/02	Payroll	Salaries	6010	Payroll 1/14/02	$2,000	
		Payroll taxes	6020		$200	
		Cash	1010			$2,200

Double-Entry Bookkeeping in Review

- Every financial transaction has two sides.

- For every transaction, at least one account is debited and one account is credited.

- Debit refers to the left side of the ledger page and credit refers to the right side of the ledger page.

- For all asset and expense accounts, a debit entry indicates an increase in the account balance and a credit entry indicates a decrease. Conversely, for all liability, net asset, and income accounts, a credit entry indicates an increase in the account balance and debit entry indicates a decrease.

- Asset and expense accounts normally have debit balances, while liability, net asset, and income accounts normally have credit balances.

- The total of all debits must equal the total of all credits

In this example we used the double-entry bookkeeping process summarized in the sidebar Double-Entry Bookkeeping in Review. For every financial transaction, at least one account was debited and one account was credited (debit refers to the left-side entry and credit refers to the right-side entry). We also assumed that the organization records financial transactions using the accrual basis of accounting discussed in Chapter Two. (In other words, income is recognized when it is earned and expenses are recognized when they are incurred. Cash basis accounting, on the other hand, recognizes income when the cash is received and expenses when the check is written.) Remembering this important difference, we have outlined the rationale behind each of the sample entries shown in Table 9, page 25.

1. The first entry recognizes the receipt of the January electric bill. Since the payment is not due until January 31, the organization is not going to write a check at this time. It simply enters the expense into the bookkeeping system by recognizing an increase to occupancy expense (debit entries increase expense accounts) and an increase to accounts payable (credit entries increase liability accounts).

2. The second entry represents payment of the December telephone bill. We assume the invoice was received earlier and entered into the bookkeeping system to recognize the expense and the obligation to pay (accounts payable). So, now that it is time to actually pay the invoice, the two accounts affected by the financial transaction are a decrease to accounts payable (debit entries decrease liability accounts) and a decrease to cash (credit entries decrease asset accounts).

3. Since this organization has an outstanding bank loan, it sends in monthly payments that do two things: (1) they pay a portion of the principal balance (debit entries decrease liability accounts); and (2) they pay interest that has accrued on the principal balance (debit entries increase expense accounts). In addition, the entry must indicate the decrease in cash when the check is written (credit entries decrease asset accounts).

4. Since the organization has only received a letter from Central Community Foundation, no cash is involved in this transaction, just the recognition that $5,000 is promised in the future. The entry reflects an increase to grants receivable (debit entries increase asset accounts) and an increase to foundation grants (credit entries increase income accounts).

5. The last sample entry recognizes the organization's semimonthly payroll. Since the organization contracts with a payroll service, the federal and state tax deposits are made automatically and therefore do not show as a withholding liability on the statement of position. That only leaves the recognition of salary and employer payroll tax expense (debit entries increase expense accounts) and a decrease in cash (credit entries decrease asset accounts).

In the example of journal entries for Northwest Housing Alliance, all transactions were entered into one journal. In this case, the journal would be referred to as a "general journal." More often, however, organizations maintain a set of journals so that information is easier to track according to: money owed by the organization (accounts payable), money owed to the organization (accounts receivable), payments made by the organization (cash disbursements), and funds received by the organization (cash receipts). All other transactions, such as depreciation expense, would be recorded in a general journal. This set of journals includes the following:

> **TIP!**
>
> **Learn how to track accounts payable and accounts receivable**
>
> Subsidiary ledgers for accounts payable and accounts receivable are not included in some computerized accounting systems. If your software does not have a payable and receivable function, you will need to track this information manually or on a computerized spreadsheet.

- An *accounts payable register* that lists all bills and invoices, plus an *accounts payable subsidiary ledger* that lists each vendor to whom the organization owes money

- A *cash disbursements journal* that lists all disbursements of funds

- An *accounts receivable register* that lists all funds owed to the organization, plus an *accounts receivable subsidiary ledger* that lists each customer, contract, or funder that owes the organization money

- A *cash receipts journal* that lists all funds received by the organization

- A *general journal* that lists all financial transactions related to accounts not included in the above journals. Examples of entries to record in the general journal include

  – Monthly depreciation expense
  – Write-off of accounts receivable (bad-debt expense)
  – Bank charges
  – Interest revenue
  – Transfers between checking and savings accounts

A blank form for each of these journals is included in Appendices A through G and can be copied for use by your nonprofit. Chapters Eight and Nine take a closer look at subsidiary ledgers and aging.

Posting to Ledger Accounts

To make information recorded in journals more usable, each item is later transferred, or posted, to a ledger. A *ledger* lists all transactions for an account in your chart of accounts. So, for instance, you will have a ledger that lists all transactions in your foundation grants account, a ledger that lists all transactions in your office supplies account, and so forth. A book or file in which all your organization's accounts are kept is called the *general ledger.*

You should post entries to ledger accounts on a regular basis. For organizations with a high volume of transactions, entries should be made daily. For smaller organizations, weekly or even biweekly entries will be sufficient.

Ledger entries should include the following pieces of information:

- Date of transaction
- Source document number if available (Example: invoice number)
- Amount of transaction
- Whether the transaction represents a debit or a credit to the account

To illustrate the process of posting to ledger accounts, we'll take the earlier example of Northwest Housing Alliance. On January 14, five transactions were made. For convenience, the journal page shown in Table 9 with its original entries has been reproduced as Table 10. Table 11 then shows these transactions recorded in individual ledger accounts. Remember, for every transaction at least one account is debited and at least one account is credited.

TABLE 10. Northwest Housing Alliance—Sample Journal Page

Date	Description of Entry	Account Name and Number		Document Number	Debit	Credit
1/14/02	January electric	Occupancy expense	7140	1/15/02 Elec	$250	
		Accounts payable	2010			$250
1/14/02	December telephone	Accounts payable	2010	12/31/02 Tele	$75	
		Cash	1010			$75
1/14/02	January loan	Loans and notes payable	2110	January-02	$500	
		Interest expense	7310		$50	
		Cash	1010			$550
1/14/02	Central Community Foundation	Grants and contributions receivable	1310	Grant reference #1032	$5,000	
		Foundation grants	4010			$5,000
1/14/02	Payroll	Salaries	6010	Payroll 1/14/02	$2,000	
		Payroll taxes	6020		$200	
		Cash	1010			$2,200

TABLE 11. Northwest Housing Alliance—Sample Ledger Accounts

Account	Cash – Checking	Account No.	1010		
Date	**Description of Entry**	**Debit**	**Credit**	**Balance**	**DR or CR***
1/1/02	Beginning balance			$8,000	DR
1/14/02	December telephone		$75	$7,925	DR
1/14/02	January loan		$550	$7,375	DR
1/14/02	Payroll		$2,200	$5,175	DR

Account	Grants and Contributions Receivable	Account No.	1310		
Date	**Description of Entry**	**Debit**	**Credit**	**Balance**	**DR or CR**
1/14/02	Central Community Foundation	$5,000		$5,000	DR

Account	Accounts Payable	Account No.	2010		
Date	**Description of Entry**	**Debit**	**Credit**	**Balance**	**DR or CR**
1/1/02	Beginning balance			$1,000	CR
1/14/02	January electric received		$250	$1,250	CR
1/14/02	Pay December telephone	$75		$1,175	CR

Account	Loans and Notes Payable	Account No.	2110		
Date	**Description of Entry**	**Debit**	**Credit**	**Balance**	**DR or CR**
1/1/02	Beginning balance			$2,500	CR
1/14/02	January loan payment	$500		$2,000	CR

Account	Foundation Grants	Account No.	4010		
Date	**Description of Entry**	**Debit**	**Credit**	**Balance**	**DR or CR**
1/14/02	Central Community Foundation		$5,000	$5,000	CR

Account	Salaries	Account No.	6010		
Date	**Description of Entry**	**Debit**	**Credit**	**Balance**	**DR or CR**
1/14/02	Payroll	$2,000		$2,000	DR

Account	Payroll Taxes	Account No.	6020		
Date	**Description of Entry**	**Debit**	**Credit**	**Balance**	**DR or CR**
1/14/02	Payroll	$200		$200	DR

Account	Occupancy Expense	Account No.	7140		
Date	**Description of Entry**	**Debit**	**Credit**	**Balance**	**DR or CR**
1/14/02	January electric	$250		$250	DR

Account	Interest Expense	Account No.	7310		
Date	**Description of Entry**	**Debit**	**Credit**	**Balance**	**DR or CR**
1/14/02	January loan	$50		$50	DR

* DR = Debit Balance   CR = Credit Balance

We have reproduced the general ledger accounts from the preceding journal entries to show how the entries impact the balance in the specific accounts. For example, the accounts payable account has two entries from January 14, one that records receipt of an invoice and one that records payment of an invoice. The accounts payable balance increased from $1,000 to $1,175.

Recording Payroll Transactions Internally

For organizations that choose to process payroll internally, additional accounts are needed to track the organization's payroll tax liabilities. For example, if Northwest Housing Alliance processed the January 14, 2002, payroll internally, it would need to make additional entries to liability accounts to reflect the following:

- Federal income tax withholding
- State income tax withholding
- Medicare withholding
- Social Security withholding

The entries made to these accounts do not change the amounts posted to salaries expense or payroll taxes expense (the employer's share) because they represent funds withheld on the employees' behalf, which the organization is obligated to deposit according to state and federal requirements.

The entry made to the cash account for the January 14, 2002, payroll will be decreased by the dollars withheld but not yet paid for these tax liabilities. When the organization submits withholding tax payments to state and federal agencies, the cash and withholding accounts will be decreased by their respective amounts.

When handling payroll internally, it is imperative that an organization make accurate and timely tax reporting and withholding deposits to stay in compliance with state and federal agencies.

One advantage of double-entry bookkeeping is the ease of determining the current balance of each account and exactly how much money has gone into and out of each account in a given period. To do this manually, total the debits and credits in each account and calculate the difference between these two amounts. A computerized system will indicate the balance automatically. As explained earlier, an account with more debits than credits is said to have a "debit balance." An account with more credits than debits is said to have a "credit balance." Remember, a debit balance does not necessarily mean that an account has a shortage or deficit. Rather, it simply means that the total of the left side of the account is greater than the total of the right side.

Based on the transactions listed earlier, Northwest Housing Alliance's account balances as of January 14 are as follows:

- Cash: $5,175 (debit)
- Grants Receivable: $5,000 (debit)
- Accounts Payable: $1,175 (credit)
- Loans and Notes Payable: $2,000 (credit)
- Foundation Grants: $5,000 (credit)
- Salaries: $2,000 (debit)
- Payroll Taxes: $200 (debit)
- Occupancy Expense: $250 (debit)
- Interest Expense: $50 (debit)

Preparing a Trial Balance

When all journal entries and ledger posts have been completed at the end of a fiscal period, or at the end of a month, a trial balance is needed to check the accuracy of the entries. A *trial balance* is a listing of all accounts and their balances in the general ledger. These balances are listed in two columns—with debit balances listed in the left column and credit balances listed in the right column. The accounts are listed in the same order as the chart of accounts, beginning with asset accounts and ending with expense accounts. If no errors have been made, the total of the debit column will equal the total of the credit column.

To illustrate, Table 12 provides a trial balance for Northwest Housing Alliance showing account balances as of January 14.

TABLE 12. Northwest Housing Alliance—Sample Trial Balance

Trial Balance as of January 14

Account	Debit	Credit
Cash	$5,175	
Accounts Receivable*	$1,000	
Grants and Contributions Receivable	$5,000	
Equipment*	$2,000	
Accumulated Depreciation*		$1,000
Accounts Payable		$1,175
Loans and Notes Payable		$2,000
Net Assets*		$6,500
Foundation Grants		$5,000
Salaries	$2,000	
Payroll Taxes	$200	
Occupancy Expense	$250	
Interest Expense	$50	
Total	**$15,675**	**$15,675**

* These account balances are carried over from the previous year.

In Table 12, the total number of debits—$15,675—equals the total number of credits—$15,675. We included not only the general ledger accounts used in the January 14 transactions but also other statement of position accounts that have a balance from the previous year—accounts receivable, equipment, accumulated depreciation, and net assets. The statement of position accounts are cumulative and do not zero out at the end of the year. We'll talk about this in detail in Chapter Five. After including all accounts, the trial balance "balances."

If the two columns of your trial balance don't match, you will need to go back and check your entries for any data entry errors. For instance: Have you entered both sides of each journal entry into at least two ledger accounts? Did you enter the numbers correctly? Do the totals of your subsidiary ledgers equal the corresponding accounts in the general ledger? Were any accounts omitted, listed twice, or placed in the wrong column of the trial balance? Do not proceed with your financial statements until your trial balance balances. This is not the time to plug in numbers to "make" it balance!

If the two columns of your trial balance don't match, you will need to go back and check your entries for any data entry errors. Do not proceed with your financial statements until your trial balance balances.

You should prepare a trial balance at the end of each month after all transactions are posted and keep a printed copy with your financial statements.

Now that your financial transactions have been properly documented and recorded, it is time to take the next step in the bookkeeping process: summarizing the information into financial statements and other reports.

Chapter Four Key Concepts

- Collect source documents for all transactions and file them in logical and consistent categories.

- Every financial transaction your organization makes should first be recorded in a journal or register. For every financial transaction, one account is debited and one account is credited.

- To make information recorded in journals more usable, each item should then be posted to ledger accounts. The general ledger shows you, in one place, all the transactions for each account listed in the chart of accounts.

- A trial balance lists all accounts and their balances. You should prepare a trial balance once a month. To balance, the total of all debit accounts should equal the total of all credit accounts.

Financial Statements 101

The previous chapter described the recording processes your organization needs to follow in order to account for its day-to-day financial transactions. The next step is to consolidate all the data from the journals, registers, and ledgers into financial statements. Financial statements are the summary products of the bookkeeping process. When properly prepared and presented, financial statements provide the reader with the information necessary to make financial decisions.

Your bookkeeping system should be designed in such a way that the resulting financial statements meet the needs of both internal and external decision makers. Internal decision makers consist of your organization's management and board of directors. For internal audiences, you are allowed a certain degree of flexibility and freedom as to what financial information is included in the statements and how they are prepared and presented. External users usually require more formal financial information prepared in accordance with generally accepted accounting principles (GAAP).

For internal purposes, your organization should produce at least two financial statements on a monthly basis: a statement of activities and a statement of position. These statements will also be prepared at year-end by your auditor for external use.

For internal purposes, your organization should produce at least two financial statements on a monthly basis: a statement of activities and a statement of position. These statements will also be prepared at year-end by your auditor for external use.

Statement of Activities

The *statement of activities* (or *income statement*) is the financial statement that shows all of your organization's income and expense activities over the course of a fiscal period (month, quarter, or fiscal year). The statement shows where income came from, how it was spent, and how much you had left (surplus) or were short (deficit). In the nonprofit world, the surplus or deficit your organization has at the end of the fiscal

STATEMENT OF
ACTIVITIES

year is called *change in net assets.* This figure will eventually be used to increase or decrease your organization's total *net assets,* a figure that appears on your statement of position.

To prepare your organization's statement of activities, you must first run a trial balance for the given period (fiscal year or fiscal year-to-date) and make sure that all accounts successfully balance. As we discussed earlier, this means that the total of all debit accounts equals the total of all credit accounts. Once this is complete, you are ready to transfer the balances of your income and expense accounts to a statement of activities report. It may be helpful to think of a statement of activities as a formal way to show how much money has flowed into and out of your organization. Instead of looking at each ledger account balance in isolation, you are summarizing account balances in a way that other readers can quickly decipher and evaluate.

Your statement of activities will include all income and expense accounts for the fiscal year-to-date. Income and expense accounts are considered *temporary accounts* because they accumulate financial information for one fiscal year only and are then closed out to zero during a year-end process called *closing entries.* We will talk about the closing process in detail in Chapter Seven.

While you will see a variety of formats among nonprofits, this statement should have certain key components:

- The heading should include your organization's name, title of the report ("Statement of Activities"), and period for which the report is being completed. Because the statement of activities analyzes financial transactions over a certain period, the date should include a beginning date and an end date.

- Income and expense accounts should be listed in the order they appear on your chart of accounts. Income account balances should be listed first, followed by expense account balances.

- At the end of your report, total expenses should be subtracted from total income to calculate *change in net assets.* If your calculation of change in net assets results in a positive number, your organization has a surplus, while if the calculation results in a negative number, your organization has a deficit. If your organization has a deficit, the negative number should be indicated with parentheses.

To illustrate, Table 13, page 35, is a statement of activities for Employment Resource Center, a fictitious nonprofit organization, for the fiscal year ending December 31, 2002.

Note that in Table 13 income and expenses are broken out into three categories: program, administration, and fundraising. Financial information is displayed by program, administration, and fundraising categories in an organization's annual audit

TABLE 13. Employment Resource Center—Statement of Activities by Cost Center for the Fiscal Year Ending 12/31/02

	Program	Administration	Fundraising	Total
Income				
Foundation grants	$94,000	$47,000	$9,000	$150,000
Individual contributions	5,800	725		6,525
Contracts	70,000			70,000
Total Income	**$169,800**	**$47,725**	**$9,000**	**$226,525**
Expenses				
Salaries	$112,500	$31,500	$6,000	$150,000
Payroll taxes	11,250	3,150	600	15,000
Employee benefits	11,250	3,150	600	15,000
Professional fees	7,500	2,500		10,000
Supplies	2,250	650	100	3,000
Telephone	750	250		1,000
Postage and shipping	750	250		1,000
Occupancy	18,750	5,250	1,000	25,000
Insurance	2,250	650	100	3,000
Interest	450	100	50	600
Bank charges	225	75		300
Depreciation	375	100	25	500
Total Expenses	**$168,300**	**$47,625**	**$8,475**	**$224,400**
Change in Net Assets	**$1,500**	**$100**	**$525**	**$2,125**

using an estimated allocation of expenses. However, some organizations prefer to set up their chart of accounts to track financial information according to individual programs and cost centers during the year, as shown in Employment Resource Center's statement of activities above. We suggest you go back to Chapter Three and look at the chart-of-account design steps again if you are considering this format for your organization.

The statement of activities is an important indicator of a nonprofit's financial health. Here are key questions this report will answer:

Did annual income cover the organization's expenses? As we will discuss in the next chapter, you should look at unrestricted funds when answering this question to get a true sense of annual income and expenses (in nonprofit accounting, temporarily restricted funds may be received or pledged in the current year, but are not available for the nonprofit to use until a later date). In the example of Employment Resource Center, all funds for the period were unrestricted. The organization showed a positive change in net assets (surplus) of $2,125.

If your organization shows a negative change in net assets (deficit) in the unrestricted category, how did it occur? What is the plan to reverse this next year? Here there are only two choices—cut expenses or increase income.

What is the organization's "money mix"? Nonprofit income falls into two general types: support (contributions) and earned revenue (contract or fee revenue). Such income comes from a variety of sources: individuals, foundations, businesses, and government agencies. At least once a year, your organization's management and board should take a good, hard look at the organization's money mix. Employment Resource Center, for instance, has a strong balance between contract revenue and foundation grants, but it has relatively little income from individual contributions. What is the mix for your organization? Can this mix be maintained in the future? Is it the right mix or should you look to other sectors for future income? What trends will affect donations, government contracts, and private fees in the coming months and years?

Key Statement of Activities Indicators

- Did annual income cover the organization's expenses?
- What is the organization's "money mix"?
- What percentage of total expenses was spent on program, administrative, and fundraising activities?

What percentage of total expenses was spent on program, administrative, and fundraising activities? Nonprofits are required to bundle these types of expenses into three explicit categories on the annual information return filed with the IRS. This bundling also makes it easier for donors to track these expenses. In Table 13, you can see that Employment Resource Center spends approximately 75 percent of its budget on program expenses (program expenses of $168,300 ÷ total expenses of $224,400 = .75). Generally speaking, program expenses should represent at least 70 percent of total expense.

For internal purposes, your statement of activities should be designed to show comparisons of *actual* income and expense amounts with *budgeted* amounts on a month-to-date and a year-to-date basis. By including budgeted amounts in the statement of activities and analyzing the differences (called "variances") between budgeted and actual, you now have a tool that helps you see if your financial plan is on track.

Table 14, page 37, is Employment Resource Center's statement of activities as of December 31, 2002, this time including budget-to-actual comparisons.

TABLE 14. Employment Resource Center—Statement of Activities with Budget-to-Actual Comparisons for the Fiscal Year Ending 12/31/02

	Actual	Budget	Variance
Income			
Foundation grants	$150,000	$145,000	$5,000
Individual contributions	6,525	6,000	525
Contracts	70,000	75,000	(5,000)
Total Income	**$226,525**	**$226,000**	**$525**
Expenses			
Salaries	$150,000	$155,000	$(5,000)
Payroll taxes	15,000	15,500	(500)
Employee benefits	15,000	15,500	(500)
Professional fees	10,000	5,000	5,000
Supplies	3,000	3,500	(500)
Telephone	1,000	750	250
Postage and shipping	1,000	1,300	(300)
Occupancy	25,000	25,000	
Insurance	3,000	2,500	500
Interest	600	500	100
Bank charges	300	300	
Depreciation	500	500	
Total Expenses	**$224,400**	**$225,350**	**$(950)**
Change in Net Assets	**$2,125**	**$650**	**$1,475**

From Table 14, we can see that Employment Resource Center did not receive as much income from contracts as projected, but it did receive more income from foundation grants than anticipated. Likewise, while the center spent more than budgeted in several categories (such as professional fees and telephone), it cut expenses in several others (such as salaries and supplies).

Statement of Position

The second financial statement you should prepare on a monthly basis is the statement of position. In one concise report, the *statement of position* (or *balance sheet*) shows your organization's financial position. It tells, at a particular point in time, what your organization owns, what it owes, and what it is worth (the difference between the first two amounts). The accounting equation that demonstrates the balancing nature of the statement of position is this:

$$\text{Assets} = \text{Liabilities} + \text{Net Assets}$$

This standard accounting formula reflects the structure of the statement of position: Assets are listed first, followed by liabilities and net assets. To balance, the total of assets must equal the total of all liabilities plus total net assets.

Assets are the economic resources your organization owns or has been promised, such as cash, accounts receivable, grants receivable, prepaid expenses, and equipment. Assets can be classified as current or noncurrent. *Current assets* can reasonably be expected to turn into cash or be consumed within a year. *Noncurrent assets* (or *fixed assets*) such as equipment are not easily converted to cash or have a useful life of several years.

Liabilities are financial obligations, or money your organization owes to others. Your organization's liabilities probably include accounts payable, accrued expenses (salaries), and loans payable. Liabilities may also be classified as *current liabilities* (those obligations due within one year) or *long-term liabilities* (debts with due dates more than twelve months in the future).

Net assets (previously known in the nonprofit sector as *fund balance*) represent the accumulation of surpluses or deficits your organization has achieved since it began operating. In other industries, this may also be referred to as "net worth" or "equity." As we discussed earlier, *change in net assets* is the term used on the statement of activities to describe the surplus or deficit experienced by the organization for a fiscal period. This figure will eventually be used to increase or decrease total net assets. If, through the years, surpluses have exceeded deficits, the net asset amount on your statement of position will be positive. If the opposite has occurred, net assets will be a negative amount and should be highlighted for board and management to take corrective action.

Statement of position accounts are considered *permanent accounts*. These accounts accumulate financial information from the beginning of the organization.

ASSETS = LIABILITIES + NET ASSETS

To create a statement of position for your organization, you must first complete a statement of activities to determine the change in net assets since the last fiscal period. Once this is complete, you are ready to transfer this calculation, plus the balances in your asset, liability, and net asset accounts, to a statement of position form.

While you will find various statement of position formats in the nonprofit world, you should make sure to include certain components:

- The heading should include your organization's name, title of the report ("Statement of Position"), and date for which the report is being completed. Because the statement of position is a snapshot of your organization at a specific point in time, the date should be a specific day, not a range or period.

- Asset, liability, and net asset accounts should be listed in the order they appear on your chart of accounts. Asset account balances should be listed first, followed by liability and net asset account balances.

To illustrate, Table 15 on page 40 is a statement of position for Employment Resource Center as of December 31, 2002.

You can see in Table 15 how the computation of change in net assets on the net asset section verifies the accuracy of the double-entry bookkeeping system. The statement of position equation holds true:

$$\text{Assets} = \text{Liabilities} + \text{Net Assets}$$

The statement of position provides important indicators of a nonprofit's financial health. So what basic indicators should you look at?

Are the organization's assets greater than its liabilities? If so, the net asset position will be positive. If negative, then the organization is in a deficit position. As of December 31, 2002, Employment Resource Center had $11,625 in assets and $3,000 in liabilities, a difference of $8,625.

Does the organization have enough cash to pay for current liabilities? Healthy organizations have at least enough cash in savings, checking, and collectable receivables to cover each dollar of outstanding current liabilities (bills due now but not yet paid). As of December 31, 2002, Employment Resource Center had a total of $5,925 in cash, plus another $4,700 in accounts and grants receivable, compared to $1,000 in current liabilities.

Is the organization "building rich" but "cash poor"? Buildings, inventory, and uncollected receivables are important assets, but they don't pay the bills. In the case of Employment Resource Center, the organization has a minimal amount of assets tied up in fixed assets.

TABLE 15. Employment Resource Center—Statement of Position as of 12/31/02

Assets		
Current Assets		
Cash – checking	$5,925	
Accounts receivable	2,200	
Grants and contributions receivable	2,500	
Total current assets		10,625
Fixed Assets		
Equipment	2,000	
Accumulated depreciation	(1,000)	
Total fixed assets		1,000
Total Assets		**$11,625**

Liabilities and Net Assets		
Current Liabilities		
Accounts payable	$1,000	
Total current liabilities		1,000
Long-Term Liabilities		
Loans/notes payable	2,000	
Total long-term liabilities		2,000
Total Liabilities		$3,000
Net Assets		
Beginning unrestricted net assets	6,500	
Change in unrestricted net assets	2,125	
Ending unrestricted net assets*		$8,625
Total Liabilities and Net Assets		**$11,625**

*Note: Employment Resource Center has no temporarily or permanently restricted net assets.

Does the organization have a payroll tax problem? If so, it will show up under the liabilities section on the statement of position. Failure to pay payroll taxes is the easiest, but most dangerous, place for a nonprofit to fall behind. Employment Resource Center does not have a problem in this area.

Has the organization received funds that are meant for future activities? If so, they'll be noted as temporarily restricted net assets, deferred revenue, or a refundable advance. To safeguard these funds, there should be a corresponding dollar amount of cash assets or accounts/contributions receivable to show that the organization is reserving these funds and has not spent them prematurely. As of December 31, 2002, Employment Resource Center did not have any temporarily restricted funds or deferred revenue.

> **Key Statement of Position Indicators**
>
> - Are the organization's assets greater than its liabilities?
> - Does the organization have enough cash to pay for current liabilities?
> - Is the organization "building rich" but "cash poor"?
> - Does the organization have a payroll tax problem?
> - Has the organization received funds that are meant for future activities? If so, are there corresponding dollar amounts in cash assets or accounts/ contributions receivables?

Other Financial Reports

While you should prepare a statement of position and statement of activities on a monthly basis, you may design other reports to meet the needs of internal decision makers or external funders. For instance, many organizations prepare a monthly cash-flow projection or a financial summary specifically for management and board that highlights key financial issues for the month and year-to-date. A financial summary form is included in Appendix I and can be customized to best fit the needs of your organization.

Chapter Five Key Concepts

- The statement of activities is the financial statement that shows all of your organization's income and expense activities from the beginning to the end of a fiscal period. The statement shows where income came from, how it was spent, and how much you had left (surplus) or were short (deficit) at the end of the fiscal period. The statement of activities is one of the most important financial statements in understanding the financial health of an organization.

- The statement of position shows your organization's financial position in one concise statement. It tells at a particular point in time what your organization owns, what it owes, and what it is worth (the difference between the first two amounts). The accounting equation for the statement of position is Assets = Liabilities + Net Assets. The statement of position provides several critical indicators of a nonprofit's financial health.

- You should prepare a statement of activities and a statement of position on a monthly basis for review by the management and board. For internal purposes, it is helpful to run a statement of activities showing budgeted-to-actual amounts on a month-to-date and year-to-date basis.

- In addition to the statement of position and statement of activities, a well-designed accounting system allows you to create customized reports to track information most helpful to management, your board, and outside constituents. It is critical to prepare financial statements in a timely fashion so that management has the opportunity to be proactive, rather than reactive, with financial decisions.

The next chapter will focus on requirements surrounding the accounting for donations to your organization.

The Importance of Donor Intent

The previous chapter looked at the two most critical financial statements you will produce for your organization: the statement of position and the statement of activities. In many regards, these statements are quite similar to statements you would find in the for-profit world. Nonprofits, however, also have specific requirements in terms of how they report financial activity and handle contributions. These requirements can be summed up in one phrase: *the importance of donor intent.*

Nonprofit Accounting Standards

In 1993, the *Financial Accounting Standards Board* (*FASB*) issued new guidelines for how nonprofits represent and classify contributions or donations. These standards, Statements of Financial Accounting Standards (SFAS) #116 and #117, contain a number of details that are too technical to present here and are best left for your auditor or certified public accountant (CPA). Several key concepts, however, are important for you to understand and track in your organization's financial system.

The biggest change brought about by these standards was the elimination of fund accounting on audited financial statements. *Fund accounting* is the process of classifying a nonprofit's resources into categories according to their nature, purpose, or restrictions. Before 1993, for instance, it was common to see unrestricted, restricted, equipment, board-designated, and endowment funds broken out on nonprofit financial statements. Some of these classifications were determined by funders (some grants, for instance, were considered restricted for a specific program), some by the board (such as board-designated reserve funds), and some by the purpose of the funds (such as equipment). As a result, it was often difficult to interpret what one organization's numbers meant when compared to the numbers of other nonprofits.

In accounting for contributions, nonprofits are now required to use categories based solely on donor intent, rather than on the purposes for which funds are used. Because of the emphasis on the donor's intent, these standards have the most impact on nonprofits dependent on pledges and multiyear grants.

FASB guidelines distinguish among three categories of net assets: unrestricted, temporarily restricted, and permanently restricted. Remember, the key distinguishing point among these is the donor's intent.

Unrestricted net assets do not have any donor restrictions imposed on them and are therefore available for general use by the nonprofit. For instance, a general operating grant does not have donor restrictions; it can therefore be used by the nonprofit for its general operating needs or other purposes as identified by the management and board, such as developing a reserve fund. Likewise, any earned revenue, such as client fees or ticket sales, is considered unrestricted. Because unrestricted net assets can be a source of confusion, we suggest you discuss this annually with your auditor.

Temporarily restricted net assets are contributions received by a nonprofit with donor restrictions that will eventually expire or will be fulfilled by an action of the organization. For instance, a nonprofit might receive a grant to fund a new program. The grant money, when first received, is considered temporarily restricted because the program has not yet begun. Once the program starts, the grant money can be released for use by the nonprofit. (An example of releasing temporarily restricted net assets is shown in Table 17, page 46.)

Permanently restricted net assets are those contributed resources on which the donor has placed a restriction that will never expire. For instance, a donor may contribute to a nonprofit's endowment. This money is therefore considered permanently restricted.

Remember, net assets are considered restricted only if the donor restricts their use. All other assets, including board-designated amounts, are legally considered unrestricted.

If you have determined that a net asset is either temporarily or permanently restricted, you will need to determine one more thing: What type of promise does the contribution reflect? Under FASB definitions, only an *unconditional promise to give* is included on nonprofit financial statements. An unconditional promise to give is a "no-strings-attached" written or oral agreement to contribute cash or other assets to another entity. In contrast, a *conditional promise to give* is a written or oral agree-

AN UNCONDITIONAL PROMISE TO GIVE IS A "NO-STRINGS-ATTACHED" AGREEMENT

ment to contribute depending on the occurrence of an uncertain future event. For instance, if a donor intends to make a contribution only if the nonprofit raises matching support from other sources, this agreement would be a conditional promise to give, and the contribution would therefore not show on the nonprofit's financial statements until after the matching amount is raised.

To illustrate how FASB standards are reflected on financial statements, we'll continue with our example of the Employment Resource Center from the last chapter. This time, however, we suppose that the organization has received a two-year grant of $20,000 for program purposes. The grant is therefore considered temporarily restricted. In year one of the grant, the statement of activities would look as shown in Table 16.

TABLE 16. Employment Resource Center—Statement of Activities for the Fiscal Year Ending 12/31/02

	Unrestricted	Temporarily Restricted	Total
Income			
Foundation grants	$150,000	$20,000	$170,000
Individual contributions	6,525		6,525
Contracts	70,000		70,000
Total Income	**$226,525**	**$20,000**	**$246,525**
Expenses			
Salaries	$150,000		$150,000
Payroll taxes	15,000		15,000
Employee benefits	15,000		15,000
Professional fees	10,000		10,000
Supplies	3,000		3,000
Telephone	1,000		1,000
Postage and shipping	1,000		1,000
Occupancy	25,000		25,000
Insurance	3,000		3,000
Interest	600		600
Bank charges	300		300
Depreciation	500		500
Total Expenses	**$224,400**		**$224,400**
Change in Net Assets	**$2,125**	**$20,000**	**$22,125**

In the next fiscal year, the center has met the first year's time-and-purpose requirement and is therefore able to release $10,000 from the temporarily restricted category. According to FASB guidelines, releasing restrictions is reported as a reclassification and is shown separately from income, expenses, gains, and losses. A separate line item called *net assets released from restrictions* is used. The statement of activities for year two of the grant would look as shown in Table 17.

Employment Resource Center's statements of position for 2002 and 2003 would look as shown in Tables 18 and 19, pages 47 and 48.

TABLE 17. Employment Resource Center—Statement of Activities for the Fiscal Year Ending 12/31/03

	Unrestricted	Temporarily Restricted	Total
Income			
Foundation grants	$150,000		$150,000
Individual contributions	6,850		6,850
Contracts	73,500		73,500
Net assets released from restrictions	10,000	(10,000)	
Total Income	**$240,350**	**$(10,000)**	**$230,350**
Expenses			
Salaries	$157,500		$157,500
Payroll taxes	15,750		15,750
Employee benefits	15,750		15,750
Professional fees	10,500		10,500
Supplies	3,150		3,150
Telephone	1,050		1,050
Postage and shipping	1,050		1,050
Occupancy	26,250		26,250
Insurance	3,150		3,150
Interest	630		630
Bank charges	315		315
Depreciation	525		525
Total Expenses	**$235,620**		**$235,620**
Change in Net Assets	**$4,730**	**$(10,000)**	**$(5,270)**

TABLE 18. Employment Resource Center—Statement of Position
as of 12/31/02

Assets

Current Assets

Cash – checking	$5,925	
Savings	20,000	
Accounts receivable	2,200	
Grants and contributions receivable	2,500	
Total current assets		30,625

Fixed Assets

Equipment	2,000	
Accumulated depreciation	(1,000)	
Total fixed assets		1,000

Total Assets		**$31,625**

Liabilities and Net Assets

Current Liabilities

Accounts payable	$1,000	
Total current liabilities		1,000

Long-Term Liabilities

Loans/notes payable	2,000	
Total long-term liabilities		2,000

Total Liabilities		$3,000

Net Assets

Beginning unrestricted net assets	6,500	
Change in unrestricted net assets	2,125	
Ending unrestricted net assets		$8,625
Beginning temporarily restricted net assets	-	
Change in temporarily restricted net assets	20,000	
Ending temporarily restricted net assets		$20,000

Total Liabilities and Net Assets		**$31,625**

TABLE 19. Employment Resource Center—Statement of Position as of 12/31/03

Assets

Current Assets

Cash – checking	$7,000	
Savings	14,725	
Accounts receivable	4,000	
Grants and contributions receivable	2,750	
Total current assets		28,475

Fixed Assets

Equipment	2,000	
Accumulated depreciation	(525)	
Total fixed assets		1,475
Total Assets		**$29,950**

Liabilities and Net Assets

Current Liabilities

Accounts payable	$3,095	
Total current liabilities		3,095

Long-Term Liabilities

Loans/notes payable	3,500	
Total long-term liabilities		3,500
Total Liabilities		$ 6,595

Net Assets

Beginning unrestricted net assets	8,625	
Change in unrestricted net assets	4,730	
Ending unrestricted net assets		$ 13,355
Beginning temporarily restricted net assets	20,000	
Change in temporarily restricted net assets	(10,000)	
Ending temporarily restricted net assets		$10,000
Total Liabilities and Net Assets		**$29,950**

Handling Contributions

When your organization receives grants, or receives contracts that have approved budgets and require special follow-up financial reporting, you will need to separately track grant and contract income and expenditures. You will at some point need to prove that funds have been used for their specified purposes.

You should first determine if your bookkeeping system can track funds by funding source (see Chapter Three on designing your chart of accounts). If yes, establish account numbers that specifically identify the funding source and use those numbers. If no, track activity for each grant and contract in a subsidiary ledger (manual or computer spreadsheet). To ensure that financial transactions are being recorded properly, educate staff and volunteers about the special account numbers or names and require that they use them. If your grants or contracts permit the organization to charge indirect expenses (space, telephone, utilities, receptionist, supervisory and managerial time, accounting expenses, and so forth) as well as direct expenses, develop a system for allocation and record these calculations in the subsidiary ledger.

Private donations

A tax-exempt organization is required to provide written acknowledgment to donors that contribute over a certain dollar amount. Since this dollar amount is subject to change, confirm the specific threshold with your CPA or audit firm.

If the donor received some value for its contribution, that cost is deducted from the gift. For instance, if a nonprofit hosts a fundraising event and charges $50 for tickets valued at $20, then the gift is considered to equal $30. Only the amount of the contribution in excess of the fair market value of the goods or services the donor received may be deducted by the donor. Your organization is required to provide that detail to individual donors at calendar year-end or at the time of the event.

Keep up on the notification requirements and develop a system to track qualifying donors. If your organization does not comply with these requirements, the IRS may impose penalties. This is a good discussion for your CPA or audit firm at year-end.

Statement of Financial Accounting Standards (SFAS) #116 and #117 at a Glance

- Unless a donor stipulates a restriction, all contributions are considered unrestricted.

- Any income earned from restricted net assets (temporary or permanent) is considered unrestricted unless the donor specifically stipulates to the contrary.

- If the restriction will be met during the current fiscal year, your organization may recognize the contribution as unrestricted when received, as long as you consistently follow this practice.

- All expenses are reported as decreases in unrestricted net assets.

- Releasing restrictions is reported as a reclassification and is shown separately from revenues, expenses, gains, and losses. When this occurs, a separate line item called "net assets released from restrictions" is used.

Funder reports

Most grants and contracts require financial reports detailing how and where the money was spent and what was accomplished with the funds. Reports may be required periodically throughout the grant/contract period or on completion. The two most important things to remember about funder reports are these: They should be accurate and they should be timely.

If your bookkeeping system has been set up to track the detail for specific contributions, the requested financial reports should be relatively easy. A computerized bookkeeping system will allow you to break out details of financial activity by funding source and, as is required by many funders, show activity for periods other than your fiscal year. A manual bookkeeping system, however, can still provide the necessary detail.

To manually track grant or contract income, you should prepare a summary sheet for each grant received (see the grant tracking form in Appendix J). Transfer key dates to a master calendar or tickler file, and track itemized expenditures on ledger paper or computerized spreadsheets. You should enter expenses as costs incurred when an invoice is received, and note when the invoice is paid. On a monthly basis, prepare a report to management on the financial status of each grant, and prepare reports on grants as required by the funder.

Chapter Six Key Concepts

- The Financial Accounting Standards Board (FASB) requires that nonprofits organize and account for financial information using categories that reflect the donor's intent. FASB distinguishes among three types of net asset categories: unrestricted, temporarily restricted, and permanently restricted. Your nonprofit must recognize all unconditional grants and pledges as income in the year the grant or pledge is made.

- Grants and contracts will often require separate reports to indicate how money was spent for that particular grant or contract. This information can be tracked in a computerized system through a funder numbering system or by assigning each grant and contract a new account number. This information can be tracked manually on ledger paper or on a computerized spreadsheet. Above all, funder reports should be accurate and timely.

The Bookkeeping Cycle

The goal of bookkeeping is to produce accurate and timely information on the financial status of your organization. Our primary focus to this point has been on various bookkeeping methods meant to ensure the accuracy of financial information. This chapter examines bookkeeping from the standpoint of frequency; in other words, ensuring the timeliness of financial information. Many bookkeeping activities need to be done on a monthly basis. Others, such as tax reporting and preparing for an audit, are done on an annual basis. Let's take a closer look now at the bookkeeping cycle throughout the course of the year.

Monthly Activities

The three essential activities of bookkeeping—documenting, recording, and summarizing financial transactions—should be completed on a regular basis. At a minimum, you should make journal and ledger entries on a monthly basis. Depending on the activity level of your organization, you may need to make these entries weekly or even daily.

On a monthly basis, you should also reconcile your statement of position accounts, subsidiary ledgers, and banking and investment accounts (see Chapters Eight and Nine for a more detailed explanation of how to reconcile these various items). These reconciliations make sure that the information on your financial statements matches subsidiary systems that track information in more detail.

It may take one to two weeks to receive documentation for monthly entries. When monthly entries and reconciliations are complete, you

TIP!

Be as smart as your accounting software

Accounting software is only as good as the knowledge of the person using it. For this reason, our book focuses primarily on the intricacies of manual bookkeeping. *It is important to note at this point that accounting software does not change the activities in the bookkeeping cycle.* The software, however, may provide tools that automate several of the processes. For instance, your software may include a bank reconciliation feature; subsidiary ledgers for accounts receivable and accounts payable; or a payroll module. In addition, the majority of accounting software provides standard formats for the two most common financial statements, the statement of position and the statement of activities.

are ready to prepare a statement of activities and statement of position. These, too, should be prepared on a monthly basis. Preparing these financial statements in a timely fashion gives board and management the opportunity to be proactive, rather than reactive, with financial decisions. Because it may take a couple of weeks to prepare financial statements, you should coordinate your board meetings to allow for timely review of financial information. Once you have prepared and distributed financial reports, no more entries should be posted to that particular month. Table 20 lists bookkeeping tasks to complete each month.

TABLE 20. Monthly Bookkeeping Tasks

Documenting and Recording

Entries

- Accounts receivable
- Accounts payable
- Cash receipts
- Cash disbursements
- Payroll
- Payroll taxes
- Noncash entries, such as depreciation and amortization
- Miscellaneous entries, such as bank charges and interest earned

Reconciliations

- All statement of position accounts
- Bank statements
- Investment accounts
- Accounts receivable to subsidiary ledger
- Fixed assets to schedule
- Accounts payable to subsidiary ledger

Summarizing

- Statement of position
- Statement of activities
- Budget-to-actual statement of activities
- Financial summary report to the board of directors

The Annual Audit

At the end of their fiscal year, most organizations will need to be independently audited, depending on their yearly income and the state in which they are located. Why do organizations need an audit? First, it's important to note that the financial statements you prepare on a monthly basis are, in accounting terms, *internal financial statements.* This means they are compiled either by in-house staff or by a financial or accounting consultant with whom an organization has contracted. These statements are designed primarily for internal use by the management and board. For external users of your organization's financial records, however, most foundations, government agencies, and banks require audited financial statements to ensure a history of appropriate spending.

An *audit* is a series of procedures followed by a professional accountant to test, on a selective basis, transactions and internal controls. Once the audit is complete, the auditor will issue an opinion on the fairness of your organization's financial statements.

Your objective is to receive an *unqualified* (or clean) *opinion* that attests to the credibility and reliability of your financial statements.

Audits are always performed by an independent outside party—a CPA—in accordance with generally accepted auditing principles. The more prepared you are for the audit, the less time the auditor will need to spend at your offices and the sooner you will receive the audited financial statements. Before the audit begins, the auditor should provide you with a list of the financial statements and records he or she will need. By preparing most, if not all, of these records and statements before the auditor arrives, the audit process is more likely to proceed smoothly. Start keeping these items in a year-end audit file so you won't have to hunt for them at the end of the year. There will be plenty to do at audit time. Table 21, page 54, provides a list of the records and statements typically required by an auditor.

Closing Entries

Once your independent audit is complete, you will be able to officially close out your fiscal year. First, make any adjustments to your accounts as indicated by your auditor (for instance, the auditor may discover an item that was not posted to the right account, or the auditor may suggest that a certain amount of your organization's accounts receivable be recognized as uncollectable). The auditor can also give you guidance regarding depreciation, releasing net assets from restrictions, and other issues that may need clarification. Finally, the auditor will indicate, based on your audit, the new balance of your net asset account. Remember, this figure is determined at year-end by the change in net assets on your audited statement of activities. (As discussed in Chapter Five, your monthly net asset balance is simply a calculation on your internal statement of position and does not reflect actual changes posted to the net asset account until the fiscal year has ended.) Through these closing entries, your accounts will be "synchronized" with audited figures, and you can proceed into the new fiscal year with confidence.

TIP!

What happens to accounts at year-end?

Income and expense accounts accumulate figures for one fiscal period only and then are brought back to zero. For this reason, they are called temporary accounts. In contrast, asset, liability, and net asset accounts start each fiscal period with the balance left over from the year before. Because they are cumulative in effect, they are referred to as permanent accounts.

At this point, most organizations perform what is called *closing the books*. Closing is the process by which all temporary accounts—income and expense accounts—are reduced to zero and the change in net assets is determined and transferred to the unrestricted net asset balance.

If you use an automated bookkeeping system, this process is a function of the system and all you have to do is go through a predefined set of steps.

It is important to remember that you should wait until all transactions have been entered before you go through the closing process.

TABLE 21. Audit Preparation Checklist

To prepare for your audit, keep these records and statements in a year-end audit file.

Documents

❑ Minutes of committee and board of directors meetings
❑ Grant and contract proposals and award letters
❑ Lease agreements
❑ Payroll-related forms and reports
❑ Insurance policies
❑ Loans and notes payable
❑ Invoices and any correspondence from your nonprofit's attorney(s)

Financial Records

❑ Bank statements and statements for all cash and investment accounts
❑ Year-to-date general ledger
❑ Financial statements and trial balance for the end of the period being audited
❑ Ledgers, journals, vendor invoices, and registers

Work Papers

For Assets:
❑ Detailed listing of accounts receivable at year-end
❑ Schedule of allowance for doubtful accounts with an explanation of how these amounts were arrived at, or details if direct charge-off method is used
❑ Depreciation schedule

For Liabilities, Including Salaries:
❑ Detailed listing of any loans and notes payable at year-end, with computations for any accrued interest and a schedule of future loan payments
❑ Schedule of salaries payable at year-end
❑ Schedule of payroll taxes and employee benefits payable at year-end
❑ Schedule of year-to-date salaries and payroll taxes
❑ Detailed schedule of employee vacation earned but not used as of year-end
❑ Schedule of temporarily restricted contributions at year-end (in the past, this might have been considered deferred revenue)

For General Expenses:
❑ Schedule of professional fees (amounts paid to attorneys, accountants, and consultants)
❑ Schedule of rent expense for the year
❑ Listing of supplies and equipment costing more than $300

For Contributions:
❑ Detailed listing of grants and contributions receivable
❑ Recap of in-kind contributions received during the year

Miscellaneous:
❑ Other schedules requested by your auditor:

_____

_____

_____

_____

_____

_____

Tax and Compliance Reporting

Even though your organization has been granted tax-exempt status as a nonprofit organization, it still must file annual returns with the IRS and with the state in which it operates. Because the tax and compliance area can be very technical and regulations and reporting requirements change constantly, we strongly recommend that you consult with competent legal and accounting advisors to ensure that you are complying with all applicable federal and state reporting requirements and procedures.

As long as your organization continues to operate according to the premises by which it obtained tax-exempt status, it does not have to pay income taxes. In lieu of preparing and filing an annual income tax return, your organization must instead file an annual information return with the IRS. The form used for this purpose is *Form 990: Return of Organization Exempt from Income Tax.*

Form 990 may be prepared internally, but most nonprofits contract with an accounting firm (usually the same firm that does their audit) to prepare all federal and state tax reporting and compliance forms. Your auditor will also help determine the percentage of expenses spent on program, management, and fundraising activities, since Form 990 requires that these expenditures be listed separately.

Once filed, your organization's Form 990 becomes a matter of public record. Except for the listing of contributors, the entire return and all attachments and schedules are available for public inspection on request through the IRS and, in most states, through the state attorney general's office. Your nonprofit is also obligated to make the return available to anyone who asks. This requirement speaks to the fact that tax-exempt nonprofits receive public support and are therefore subject to public accountability.

Proper preparation and timely filing of Form 990 is necessary to maintain your organization's good standing with the IRS. In addition to federal filing and reporting requirements, most states require nonprofit organizations to register with and submit financial reports to one or more state agencies. This is a good discussion to have with your audit firm at year-end, to ensure your organization is in compliance with federal and state reporting requirements.

We are now going to shift our focus from how to track financial activity to how to safeguard your organization's assets. The procedures that safeguard assets are known as *internal controls,* the topic of Chapter Eight.

TIP!

Understand unrelated business income

If your organization engages in activities that generate *unrelated business income,* it may be required to pay *unrelated business income tax* (UBIT). For example, if your organization has a shop in which both educational and gift items are sold, the money it receives from the sale of gifts may be taxable as unrelated business income.

The IRS has three criteria for unrelated business activity:

1. The activity is not substantially related to the purpose for which the nonprofit received tax-exempt status

2. The activity must be a trade or business

3. The activity must be regularly carried on

All three of the above criteria must be present for an activity to be labeled unrelated business activity. If the criteria are present, your organization is subject to UBIT on any net income generated by this activity. See your CPA or audit firm for clarification. You can also download information on UBIT from the IRS web site at www.irs.gov.

TIP!

Stay current with payroll withholdings and taxes

While specific filing requirements vary from state to state, your organization is required to submit employee state and federal withholding taxes, Medicare and Social Security (FICA) taxes, and various payroll tax reports on a regular basis. Failure to comply can result in significant financial penalties.

Chapter Seven Key Concepts

• On a monthly basis, you should complete all journal and ledger entries, reconcile statement of position accounts, subsidiary ledgers, and bank and investment accounts, and prepare internal financial statements.

• The more prepared you are for your annual audit, the more likely the audit will proceed smoothly. Start keeping records and statements in a year-end audit file to save yourself work at the end of the year.

• Because the tax and compliance area can be very technical and regulations and reporting requirements change constantly, we strongly recommend that you consult with competent legal and accounting advisors to ensure that you are complying with all applicable federal and state reporting requirements and procedures, including preparation of Form 990.

Internal Controls Part I:
Protecting What You Own

So far this book has discussed the principles and techniques of analyzing, planning, and reporting nonprofit financial activity. But safeguarding the assets of your organization is at least as important as understanding their use. Board and management have a primary responsibility to ensure that the assets entrusted to them are not diverted from their proper purpose through error, loss, or theft. The procedures that safeguard assets are called *internal controls.*

Internal controls serve several purposes. They safeguard assets, produce accurate financial data, contribute to efficient operations, and promote compliance with board policy, grant restrictions, and other regulations. For instance, timely bank reconciliations allow your organization to quickly identify unusual payments or charges. The double-entry system of bookkeeping ensures that financial transactions are recorded properly. Segregation of duties organizes tasks efficiently and with appropriate safeguards. Assets such as restricted contributions are guarded through a careful tracking system. While internal controls may not be a "glamorous" topic, they are nonetheless critical to the financial well-being of your organization.

IT IS IMPORTANT TO SAFEGUARD THE ASSETS OF YOUR ORGANIZATION

Many managers don't institute a system of internal controls because they feel it would be insulting to their employees. But remember, good internal control systems can benefit employees. If any shortages or discrepancies appear, an employee working under a good system of internal controls is more easily protected from suspicion. When shortages appear in an organization without good internal controls, then everyone becomes a suspect, which can be personally as well as professionally damaging.

Ideally, bookkeeping responsibilities will be divided among different employees. For this reason, internal control techniques may be difficult for some nonprofits that operate with a very small staff. Nonetheless, it is possible to set up an internal controls system within the smallest of operations since even a one-person operation has a board of directors that can handle certain controlling functions.

Budgets and Financial Statements

While most of our discussion on internal controls will focus on various processes and procedures, we'll first look at the critical role that budgets and financial statements serve in a good internal control system.

A *budget* expresses an organization's goals and objectives in dollars and cents. In addition to serving as a planning tool, the budget also fulfills another critical function: to provide internal control. If used appropriately, this tool can provide management an early warning sign in the event that the organization's financial goals are not being met. The key here is to incorporate your budget into the ongoing financial reporting process. Don't assume that just preparing and approving the budget is enough. Use the budget to compare against actual financial activity on a month-to-date and year-to-date basis and investigate any variances as they arise. To the extent possible, explain variances to the board and management and indicate whether they are a one-time or ongoing problem.

Financial statements, such as the statement of position and statement of activities, likewise allow board and management to evaluate the organization's financial position. When these reports are produced in an accurate and timely manner, management can respond in a proactive manner and adjust plans and strategies accordingly.

There are several ways to ensure that financial statements provide appropriate internal control:

- Design financial statements so that they provide meaningful information to aid in decision making.
- Produce statements on a regular basis for review by board and appropriate staff. Statements for the prior month should be available for the board meeting in the month immediately following.
- Internal statements should compare actual financial activity to the budget. Highlight critical variances between budgeted and actual amounts and describe action steps that will be taken in response. Also, identify anticipated or potential variances and related contingency plans.

Why Internal Controls?

- Safeguard your organization's assets.
- Produce accurate financial data.
- Contribute to efficient operations.
- Promote compliance with board policy, grant restrictions, and other regulations.

Segregation of Duties

Your independent auditor will always ask about your organization's internal controls and comment if they are reasonable for an organization your size. One of the cornerstones of internal controls is the *segregation of duties*. In other words, the auditor will look to see that responsibilities are assigned to personnel so that no one person controls all aspects of a financial transaction. In particular, organizations should separate responsibilities for the receiving and spending of resources from the financial record-keeping and reconciliation functions.

Let's look at the basic principles and procedures for your most common financial transactions. The rest of this chapter focuses on transactions related to your organization's assets. The next chapter examines ways to safeguard your organization's expenditures and liabilities. Because we cover so many issues in these two chapters, you should plan to refer to them many times as you design and implement a system that works well for your organization.

> **TIP!**
>
> **Don't lose sight of internal controls when your systems are automated**
>
> Be aware that computerized accounting systems can undermine the accuracy and availability of accounting records. Fewer people are involved in transactions, financial data are more concentrated, and there is less visible evidence in the automated accounting process. Make sure that you still have appropriate segregation of duties; limit the number of staff that can access your accounting computer; and don't become lazy in maintaining your documentation.

Receiving Cash and Checks

To maintain adequate segregation of duties, the same person should *not*

- Receive and log cash and checks
- Prepare, make, and record the deposit entry
- Receive the bank statement

Segregation of duties is possible even in the smallest of organizations. For instance, the executive director could log and endorse checks, a contract bookkeeper could make deposits, and the board treasurer could receive the bank statement and review reconciliations.

Here are other procedures to follow in receiving cash and checks:

- Log all incoming cash and checks. Indicate the name of the payer, the amount of payment, and the date received (see Appendix F for a cash receipts journal form).
- Restrictively endorse all incoming checks (for example, write "For Deposit Only").
- Bundle checks and cash for deposit, along with corresponding cover letters and explanatory backup information, and put them in a secure place.
- Don't spend incoming cash for other purposes—deposit it intact.
- Make timely bank deposits, either at regular intervals or when funds accumulated for deposit reach a predetermined threshold amount.

Preparing the Deposit

Several steps should be taken to ensure adequate internal controls in the process of preparing deposits:

- Photocopy all checks and record on the copies key identifying information about payments.
- Prepare the deposit by listing all checks and cash received on a deposit slip.
- Photocopy the deposit slip and attach the check copies, cash detail, and backup documentation that accompanied the payments.
- Make the deposit at the bank and obtain a receipt showing the correct amount and date of the deposit.
- Attach the bank receipt to a duplicate deposit slip and supporting documents.
- Record the deposit in the check register with the date and amount.
- Determine if a transfer from checking to savings or other investment account is needed.
- Place the duplicate deposit slip and attached documents in the transaction file.

Reconciling Your Bank Statement

Every organization should promptly reconcile its monthly bank statement with internal records of cash on hand. To start with, your organization should designate a person to receive the bank statement every month. This person should be different from the one who handles cash disbursement, cash receipt processing, and reconciling the bank statement. Some organizations have a board member receive the bank statement. This person should

- Open the statement and go through the checks looking for any unusual amounts or payees, including any person on a payroll check who is not familiar or who no longer works at the organization. Review questions with the check writer.
- Initial and date the bank statement after review and pass it to the person who does the reconciliation.

Once the statement has been received, you are ready to reconcile your account.

- Put the checks in numerical order.
- Compare your bank statement to your check register. Note which checks, deposits, and withdrawals have cleared your bank account.
- Subtract from your general ledger cash account any service, miscellaneous, or automatic charges shown on the bank statement. Add to your general ledger any interest earned as shown on your bank statement.
- Total the amount of checks and withdrawals that have not yet cleared your bank account. Subtract this amount from the ending balance on your bank statement. Add

the total of deposits made but not shown on the statement. This final balance should be the same as the cash balance listed in the check register for the month-end. Your check register balance should also equal your general ledger cash account.

- File the bank statement with your balanced reconciliation form (see the bank statement reconciliation form in Appendix K) in your transaction file.

Accounts Receivable

Accounts receivable are created when the organization has provided goods or services that will be paid for later. To maintain proper segregation of duties, the same person should *not*

- Set pricing for goods and services
- Receive payments
- Send billings and maintain the accounts receivable records

Here are procedures to follow to ensure proper internal controls for accounts receivable:

- Clearly establish authorized prices for services and goods and communicate the price schedule to those responsible for billing.
- Create a process for changing authorized prices.
- Promptly communicate authorized changes in pricing.
- Make no exceptions to authorized pricing without approval by an appropriate manager or director.
- Develop a system to record performance of services or the sale of goods.
- Send the service/sale records to another person for billing.
- Use serially prenumbered invoices for billing.
- Maintain a subsidiary ledger of billed accounts receivable (see Appendix E for an accounts receivable subsidiary ledger), including:
    - Name of person or organization billed
    - Address and phone for account
    - Date initially billed
    - Amount billed
    - Invoice number
    - Date follow-up invoices are sent
    - Date payments are received
    - Balances still due after partial payments
- Periodically balance the accounts receivable subsidiary ledger with the general ledger.

- Take follow-up action on overdue invoice balances on a timely basis.
- Periodically review unpaid accounts to determine if they are collectable.
- Obtain authorization by proper personnel before writing off uncollectable accounts.

Aging of Accounts Receivable

Aging of accounts receivable is the process of analyzing the age of all open invoices owed to the organization. At least quarterly, you should set up and review an *aging of accounts receivable*. This process will provide information on how long ago you actually sent an invoice to your customer.

- List open invoices for each customer by billing date and enter in the total column plus one of four columns specifying the age of the invoice (see Appendix E for an accounts receivable subsidiary ledger):
  - Total (all outstanding invoices for each customer)
  - Current (today to 30 days old)
  - Over 30 (31 days old to 60 days old)
  - Over 60 (61 days old to 90 days old)
  - Over 90 (any open amounts over 90 days old)

- Follow a set procedure for sending statements to customers with overdue invoices and accounting for any receivables determined to be uncollectable.

Accounting for Bad Debts

The longer a receivable is outstanding, the greater the chance that it will not be paid in full. If your organization has a significant accounts receivable balance, you should develop a system to account for these "bad debts" and reduce the accounts receivable value over time.

Bad debt may be recorded in one of two ways: the direct charge-off method or the allowance method. The *direct charge-off method* evaluates each receivable on a case-by-case basis to determine the likelihood of collecting it. When you determine that your organization won't be able to collect the receivable, the entire amount is charged off as bad debt. You would debit your *bad debt expense account* and credit *accounts receivable* for the entire amount. An entry should also be made in the *accounts receivable subsidiary ledger* to reduce the balance by that amount.

The direct charge-off method results in reducing your accounts receivable balance and recognizing an expense at the specific time you realize an account will not be collected. Organizations with a history of minimal bad debt often use this method.

The *allowance method* reduces the value of your receivables by a certain percentage each month. This rate uses a predetermined formula based on industry standards or the experience of your particular organization. The advantage of this method is that it reduces the chance that your organization will take an unexpected "hit" when a receivable is deemed not collectable. On a monthly basis, you should debit your *bad debt expense account* and credit the *allowance for doubtful accounts* by your predetermined amount.

The allowance method requires a second step once you determine that an outstanding receivable will not be collected. At that point you will need to remove it from your financial records. You should debit your *allowance for doubtful accounts* and credit the *accounts receivable account* for the full amount of the receivable. You should also make an entry in the accounts receivable subsidiary ledger to reduce the balance by that amount.

At least once a year, if not more frequently, you should determine if the allowance for doubtful accounts is adequate compared to your aging of accounts receivable. Use this determination to adjust your allowance for doubtful accounts.

Work with your auditor to determine which method is best for your organization. Once determined, you should consistently follow a set procedure for determining uncollectable accounts receivable.

Petty Cash

Petty cash is a fund established to meet the minor cash operating needs of the organization. Use of petty cash should be short term and carefully controlled. The same person should not handle petty cash and reconcile the fund.

- Set up the petty cash account for a specified, authorized amount equal to the needs of the organization. Generally speaking, this fund should be very small in amount.
- Set a ceiling on the amount of expenditures that can be made using petty cash.
- Make petty cash the responsibility of only one person and keep it in a secure place.
- Document petty cash disbursements using a voucher or other record that indicates the person to whom cash was advanced, the date cash was advanced, and the purpose of the advance.
- Clearly notify employees that they must return receipts equal to the amount of a petty cash advance within a specific period.
- Match returned vendor receipts to the appropriate voucher. Receipts should equal the amount of petty cash advanced on each voucher.
- Balance the account monthly. Cash plus vouchers with attached receipts should equal the required account balance.

- Enter disbursements from petty cash in their appropriate expense categories.
- Do not issue petty cash in return for IOUs or personal checks or for any unauthorized purpose.
- To replenish the petty cash fund, use an approved check request with attached receipts totaling the amount of the replenishment request.

Inventories

If your organization maintains an *inventory* of educational materials, books, or other goods, internal controls are needed.

- Secure the inventory and designate one person to have "custody" and be responsible for quantities and the condition of goods on hand.
- Establish and communicate a system of approval for both withdrawals from inventory and purchases for inventory.
- Segregate the functions of purchasing inventory from inventory custody and record keeping.
- Maintain a subsidiary ledger to track the amount and value of inventory coming into the organization and the amount and value of inventory going out.
- Periodically reconcile the subsidiary inventory records to the general ledger.
- Periodically take a physical count of the inventory. The count should be performed by someone other than the person responsible for inventory custody.

Fixed/Capital Assets

Small start-up nonprofits may not initially have any *fixed* or *capital assets,* such as land, buildings, or equipment that has a relatively long useful life. As your organization grows, however, and you acquire these types of assets, you should observe the following steps to ensure adequate internal controls:

- Establish a board-approved definition of a capital asset as opposed to an annual expense.
- Establish a board-approved depreciation policy.
- Obtain advance board approval for capital purchases over a board-determined dollar amount.
- Obtain advance board approval for any borrowing to acquire capital assets.
- Establish a subsidiary record to track capital assets, including:
  - Date the asset was acquired
  - Brief description of the asset

- Asset location
- Amount paid for the asset
- Estimated useful life of the asset
- Annual depreciation amount

• Periodically balance the subsidiary capital asset record with the general ledger.

• Obtain appropriate insurance on the organization's capital assets. This should be updated annually.

• Place an identifying tag on each incoming capital asset so that it can be easily inventoried.

• Periodically check the fixed asset record by making a physical count.

• Establish procedures for receiving and recording gifts of capital assets.

• Establish procedures to govern the disposal of capital assets.

Depreciation

An organization's depreciation policy should be set by the board of directors and reviewed by the organization's audit firm. Depreciation is the process by which the cost of a fixed asset is expensed over its useful life. The vast majority of nonprofits use a simple *straight line depreciation method*. This method recognizes equal amounts of depreciation over the course of the asset's useful life. For example, if you purchase $3,600 worth of computer equipment, determined to have a useful life of three years (thirty-six months), the monthly depreciation expense would be equal to the cost ($3,600) divided by the useful life in months (thirty-six months), which equals $100/month. On a monthly basis, then, you would debit *depreciation expense* by $100 and credit *accumulated depreciation* by $100.

Since depreciation does not involve the transfer of cash, some organizations wonder why it is necessary to recognize it as an expense. Depreciation allows your organization to show that your equipment and fixtures decrease in value each year. Organizations that budget and fully fund their depreciation expense each year are, in essence, creating a replacement reserve for future purchases.

When purchasing fixed assets, assign each purchase an asset type (computer, furniture, etc.) and record the purchase on the fixed/capital asset schedule. Each asset type should be assigned a useful life according to your organization's depreciation policy, from which you can determine your annual depreciation entries.

Depreciation entries should be made at least annually to adjust the value of fixed/capital assets. To more accurately reflect the organization's activities and position, we recommend that you recognize depreciation expense monthly.

Organizations that budget and fully fund their depreciation expense each year are, in essence, creating a replacement reserve for future purchases.

Disposition of Fixed/Capital Assets

Although fixed or capital assets such as equipment may have a relatively long useful life, at some point in time they break, wear out, or become obsolete. When your organization needs to dispose of obsolete or surplus capital assets, follow these guidelines:

- Obtain appropriate authorization for disposal according to board-determined policies.
- Determine the book value of the capital assets at the time of disposal.
- Record in the appropriate ledgers any capital asset sale and gain or loss.

Below are sample entries of the sale and disposition of assets. Entries to the left indicate debit entries. Entries to the right represent credit entries.

Sale of asset: gain

Imagine that your organization purchased a set of office furniture valued at $1,000. Since then, the furniture has been fully depreciated (a total of $1,000 has been credited to the accumulated depreciation account). Your organization then sells the furniture for $100. This represents a gain (income) of $100, since your organization is receiving money for an asset that no longer has any value in your books. Following is an entry for recognizing the receipt of cash and removing the asset from your organization's books. Notice we have listed the accounts that will be debited first and then the accounts that will be credited.

	Debit	Credit
Cash	$100	
Accumulated Depreciation	$1,000	
Office Equipment		$1,000
Misc. Income		$100

Sale of asset: loss

Taking the previous example, suppose that the value of the furniture has been depreciated by $800 instead of the full $1,000 amount. Your organization then sells the furniture for $100. This represents a loss (expense) of $100, since your organization is receiving $100 less than the $200 value of the asset in your books.

	Debit	Credit
Cash	$100	
Accumulated Depreciation	$800	
Misc. Expense	$100	
Office Equipment		$1,000

Disposition of asset: fully depreciated

From a slightly different angle, suppose that your organization purchased the set of office furniture valued at $1,000. Since then, the furniture has been fully depreciated (a total of $1,000 has been credited to the accumulated depreciation account). Instead of selling the furniture, however, your organization decides to simply throw it away, since it's in rough condition. Your entries would be as follows:

	Debit	Credit
Accumulated Depreciation	$1,000	
Office Equipment		$1,000

Disposition of asset: partially depreciated

Taking this same example, consider that the value of the furniture has been depreciated by $800 instead of the full $1,000 amount. When your organization throws the furniture away, the $200 difference would be posted as an expense.

	Debit	Credit
Accumulated Depreciation	$800	
Misc. Expense	$200	
Office Equipment		$1,000

All of the preceding examples result in removing the asset from your organization's financial records. The variables all have to do with the depreciation amount recorded on the asset and whether cash was involved in the transaction.

SALE OF FIXED/CAPITAL ASSETS

Chapter Eight Key Concepts

- Internal controls serve four main purposes. They safeguard assets, produce accurate financial data, contribute to efficient operations, and promote compliance with board policy, grant restrictions, and other regulations.

- Budgets and financial statements serve an important role in an internal control system. Compare actual financial activity against the budget on a month-to-date and year-to-date basis and investigate any variances as they arise. Financial statements, such as the statement of position and statement of activities, likewise allow board and management to evaluate the organization's financial position and provide an early warning sign in the event that financial goals are not being met.

- It is possible to maintain appropriate segregation of duties within even the smallest of operations if the board of directors handles certain controlling functions.

Internal Controls Part II:
Protecting Your Expenditures and Liabilities

We continue our discussion of internal controls with a look at transactions related to your organization's expenditures and liabilities.

Accounts Payable

Accounts payable are created when the organization has received goods or services but has not yet paid for them. To maintain appropriate segregation of duties, the same person should not

- Approve purchase orders/purchases
- Make purchases
- Receive the vendor invoice and maintain accounts payable records

A *purchase order* is a signed document authorizing a supplier to charge purchases to an organization's account. Purchase orders have two primary purposes: to protect the organization from improper use of its credit, and to estimate accounts payable for which an invoice has not yet been issued.

Following are steps to ensure appropriate internal controls for purchasing:

- Establish a board-approved purchase authorization policy that includes who can authorize purchases and at what dollar amount, and the number of signatures required for purchases above a certain dollar threshold.
- Require three competitive bids for items to be purchased unless approved vendor lists or supply catalogs are used.
- Develop a policy statement with regard to purchasing conflicts of interest, including employee-vendor and board member-vendor relationships.

- Require advance approval for all purchases. A purchase order should include
  - Name of person (and department if appropriate) ordering the goods/services
  - Vendor name and address
  - Description of goods/services ordered
  - Estimated cost of goods/services
  - Brief description of organizational use for goods/services
  - Budget category to which goods/services should be charged
  - Authorizing signature(s)

- Before approving a purchase order, review the request against the amount remaining in the appropriate budget category to be sure funds will not be spent in excess of the approved budget.

- Send copies of approved purchase orders to both the person who will pay the bills and the person who will receive incoming goods.

- Require that incoming goods be received by someone other than the person who ordered the goods.

- Establish who will decide whether to approve receipt of incoming goods if no purchase order is on file. This should not be the person who ordered the goods.

- Count and inspect all incoming items.

- Obtain a receipt, shipping slip, or other receiving document for all incoming items that are accepted. Note on receiving documentation any problems with the incoming order.

- Send receiving documentation with noted comments to the person who pays the bills.

- Before paying for purchases, make sure the purchase order, receiving documents, and invoice match.

Accounts Payable Records

Following are steps to ensure appropriate internal controls for accounts payable records:

- Route all incoming invoices directly to the person who will maintain the accounts payable records.

- Match incoming invoices with purchase authorizations and receiving documents on hand.

- Seek information about invoices for which no documentation is on hand. Who authorized the purchase and for what purpose?

- Promptly discuss with vendors any questions about amount or timing of invoices. Document these discussions and attach comments to the appropriate invoice.

- Maintain a subsidiary ledger of accounts payable (see Appendix B for an accounts payable subsidiary ledger), which records the
    - Name, address, and phone of the vendor
    - Invoice number (to avoid duplicate payments)
    - Brief description of goods or services purchased
    - Purpose of purchase
    - Date invoice received
    - Total amount of invoice
    - Amount of payment due
    - Date payment is due
- Hold invoices with attached authorization documentation in a pending file organized by the date payments are due.
- Periodically balance subsidiary accounts payable with the general ledger.
- Periodically age unpaid accounts.

Aging of Accounts Payable

Aging of accounts payable is the process of analyzing the age of all open invoices owed by your organization to each of its vendors. At least quarterly, you should set up and review an *aging of accounts payable.* This process will provide information on how old your organization's vendor debt has become.

List open invoices for each vendor by billing date and enter in the total column plus one of four columns specifying the age of the invoice (see Appendix B for an accounts payable subsidiary ledger):

1. Total (all outstanding invoices for each vendor)
2. Current (today to 30 days old)
3. Over 30 (31 days old to 60 days old)
4. Over 60 (61 days old to 90 days old)
5. Over 90 (any open amounts over 90 days old)

AGING OF ACCOUNTS PAYABLE

30 DAYS   60 DAYS   90 DAYS   120 DAYS

Paying the Bills

There are several steps to ensure appropriate internal controls for bill paying:

- Establish a board-approved schedule of check-signing authority, including who can sign checks, the authority ceilings for each check signer, and the number of signatures required on checks over a certain dollar amount.

- Clearly segregate the functions of payment authorization, processing of payment requests, and check signing.

- Use prenumbered checks.

- Control access to blank check stock and account for all returned or voided checks.

- Use the accounts payable records to ensure that bills are paid in a timely fashion, taking advantage of available discounts and avoiding late payment penalties.

- Use purchase authorizations, receiving documentation, and personal follow-up to ensure that payment is not made on invoices for which the goods and services have not been received or are not satisfactory.

- Prepare a *check request* for each payment to be made. The check request, or an approval on an invoice, should include the following information:
  - Date of request
  - Name of person requesting a check be written
  - Name and address of vendor to be paid
  - Brief description of purchase
  - Amount of the check
  - Budget category to be charged
  - Approval signature(s) if no purchase authorization was used

- Type each check and attach the invoice, completed check request, purchase authorization, and receiving documentation if applicable.

- Do not write checks to "cash" or sign blank checks in advance.

- Bring the checks and backup documents to the authorized person(s) for review and signature.

- Record signed check dates and amounts in the check register and determine if cash needs to be transferred from savings to checking.

- Promptly mail the check, along with the appropriate invoice copy, to the vendor. Don't hold checks before mailing.

- File a check copy, the check request, an invoice copy, the purchase authorization, and the receiving documentation in a transaction file.

Employee Advances

If your organization advances money to employees for direct client expenses or to make purchases for the organization, the following controls should be in place:

- To maintain appropriate segregation of duties, the same person should not
    - Approve an advance
    - Receive the advance
    - Maintain the records on advances

- Set a ceiling on the total amount an employee may receive as an advance.

- Ensure that employees have submitted the receipts to document and finalize one advance before they receive another.

- When funds are issued to an employee, immediately create a record of the advance in the subsidiary receivables ledger.

- Review the employee advance record monthly and provide information about unreturned advances to the appropriate person.

- Clearly notify employees that failure to either provide proper receipts or return advanced money in a timely fashion will be considered unauthorized use of agency funds. Some agencies have a policy that deducts these funds from an employee's salary after a certain time expires.

Employee Travel

If you have employees who travel, you will need to establish guidelines for travel expenditure:

- Identify who can authorize employee travel for reimbursement.
- Clearly communicate that only preapproved travel is eligible for reimbursement.
- Establish and communicate policies for reimbursement of
    - Mileage
    - Airfare
    - Ground transportation
    - Food
    - Lodging

- Establish and communicate policies about reimbursement of other expenses. For example, are you willing to reimburse non-work-related items such as alcoholic beverages, telephone, and in-room movies?
- Set a time frame within which travel reimbursement requests must be submitted.

Payroll

Employment law is a complicated field with requirements that vary from state to state. Whether you choose to maintain your payroll function in-house or use a payroll service, the following steps should be taken to ensure proper internal controls:

- Do not pay an employee without having written authorizations on file governing rates of pay, withholdings, and deductions.

- Do not change an employee's status or wage rate without proper authorization. Record changes in employment status in employee personnel files.

- Only pay employees for time actually worked. Change your payroll cycle rather than estimate hours worked.

- Prepare the payroll after receipt of approved time sheets and based on those reports.

- Prepare employee earnings records showing current and cumulative withholding amounts including Medicare, Social Security, federal withholding, state withholding, and any other deductions.

- Prepare checks for net payroll amount and handle in a manner similar to normal bill paying.

- Record the payroll gross and withholding amounts on individual earnings records.

- Become knowledgeable about the laws governing minimum wage, employment taxes, and compensation for overtime, and the rules for determining whether employees are *exempt* or *non-exempt* from overtime laws. Also, be careful about using the *independent contractor* employment category even though it can minimize employment taxes. Because employment status is a confusing area for many organizations, we suggest you discuss this with your auditor or the oversight agency in your state.

- Require prior authorization before overtime is worked and track overtime use.

- Track use of vacation, sick leave, holiday, or other personal time relative to time earned. Regularly communicate to employees about unused sick, holiday, vacation, or personal time available to them.

- Clearly segregate the functions of hiring/wage-level authorization, payroll approval and preparation, and payroll check distribution.

Other Internal Control Issues

We have covered several major areas of financial transactions requiring varying degrees of internal control. Here are some final internal control issues:

- Document all financial policies in a manual.

- Establish procedures to govern the maintenance of accounting records, including

  - Guidelines to ensure that all journal entries have adequate support and explanation.

  - Maintenance of records in a limited access area.

  - Accounting for all serially numbered records that are used, spoiled, and unused.

  - Taking action in connection with missing records.

- Maintain an organizational chart that sets forth the actual lines of authority and responsibility.

- Purchase fidelity bond insurance to cover employees who handle money.

- Review all agency insurance policies annually to ensure adequate coverage is provided.

- Ensure that timely minutes are prepared after every board meeting. Minutes should include

  - Complete list of who attended and who did not.

  - List of all official actions taken, including the text of all motions made, who made and seconded each motion, whether motions passed or did not pass, and vote count.

  - List of all other actions taken by the board.

- Put procedures in place to document receipt of in-kind contributions and record them in the financial system as appropriate.

- Establish a board-approved policy regarding contracts, including who may commit the organization to contracts, and at what dollar amount contracts must be preapproved by the board.

- Establish a system for recording and filing all agency contracts.

- Prohibit loans to employees or board members.

If Chapters Eight and Nine have introduced some new procedures for you, it may be helpful to go through the internal controls checklist in Table 22, pages 76-77. In addition, Appendices L and M contain an activity to help your organization achieve segregation of duties. See if you can create an effective system of internal controls using your staff or if you will have to involve board members too.

TABLE 22. Internal Controls Checklist

Cash Receipts

- ❑ Cash receiving, processing, recording, and bank statement reconciliation functions are clearly segregated.
- ❑ Checks received are listed individually on a control sheet for comparison with the bank deposit ticket.
- ❑ Checks are restrictively endorsed (stamped "For Deposit Only") by the person opening the mail.
- ❑ Cash is deposited intact (without any "temporary" withdrawals, say for petty cash purposes) in a bank account and on a timely basis.
- ❑ Duplicate deposit slips are prepared.
- ❑ Validated deposit slips are received from the bank and attached to the deposit detail.

Cash Disbursements

- ❑ Authorization, processing, check-signing, recording, and bank statement reconciliation functions are clearly segregated.
- ❑ Persons authorized to approve expenditures are clearly identified.
- ❑ Expenditures are approved in advance by authorized persons (such as through a purchase order system).
- ❑ Invoices or requests for expenditures are supported by appropriate documentation and approval(s).
- ❑ Supporting documents are canceled (i.e., stamped PAID) to prevent subsequent use.
- ❑ All cash disbursements are made by prenumbered checks.
- ❑ The person processing checks keeps a record of cash disbursements.
- ❑ Two signatures are required on each check or on all checks over a certain dollar amount.
- ❑ Signed checks are mailed promptly.
- ❑ Checks are controlled and accounted for with safeguards for returned and voided checks.
- ❑ Blank checks are properly controlled and securely stored.
- ❑ Checks written to "cash" are prohibited.
- ❑ Signing checks in advance is prohibited.
- ❑ Bank statements are reconciled monthly.

Payroll

- ❑ The personnel authorization, payroll approval and preparation, payroll check distribution, record-keeping, and bank statement reconciliation functions are clearly segregated.
- ❑ Changes in employment (new hires and terminations), salaries, wage rates, and payroll deductions are authorized by proper personnel.
- ❑ Policies and procedures are in place for accounting for vacations, holidays, and sick leave.
- ❑ Changes in employment status are recorded in employee personnel files.
- ❑ Time sheets for each employee are maintained and authorized by proper personnel.
- ❑ Payroll checks are always prepared after receipt of approved time sheets and based on those reports.
- ❑ All disbursements are made by prenumbered checks.
- ❑ The summary of the payroll register is posted to the general ledger on a timely basis.

Accounts Receivable

- ❑ Changes in prices for services or products are promptly communicated.
- ❑ Billing is done by serially prenumbered invoices.
- ❑ The subsidiary receivables ledger is periodically balanced with general ledger control accounts.
- ❑ Follow-up action is taken on overdue balances.
- ❑ Collections are promptly recorded in receivables records.
- ❑ Outstanding accounts are properly analyzed to determine if they are collectable and periodically aged.
- ❑ The write-off of uncollectable accounts is authorized by proper personnel.

Accounts Payable

- ❑ Authorization, processing, recording, and payment functions are clearly segregated.
- ❑ All approved invoices are promptly recorded in the accounts payable register to establish control for payment.

Accounts Payable (continued)

❑ Unpaid invoices are maintained in a distinct unpaid invoice file.

❑ Statements from vendors are regularly compared with open invoice files.

❑ Invoices from unfamiliar or unusual vendors are reviewed and approved for payment by authorized personnel who are independent of the invoice processing function.

❑ Payments are promptly recorded in the accounts payable register to avoid double payment.

❑ The accounts payable register is periodically reconciled with the general ledger by a person independent of the invoice processing function.

❑ The organization obtains competitive bids for items whose cost exceeds a specified dollar amount.

Inventory

❑ Inventory purchasing and custodial, processing, and record-keeping functions are clearly segregated.

❑ Responsibility for inventory is established and appropriate safeguards are maintained.

❑ The receipt, transfer, and withdrawal of inventory items are promptly recorded in the inventory records. Quantity records of inventory items are maintained.

❑ Inventory records are periodically reconciled with the general ledger.

❑ A physical inventory is periodically taken by persons independent of custody and processing functions.

Fixed Assets

❑ Fixed asset purchases are permitted only if preapproved by the board.

❑ Borrowing for fixed asset purchases is limited to specific authorization by the board.

❑ The organization has established policies covering capitalization and depreciation.

❑ Detailed records are maintained showing the asset values of individual units of property and equipment.

❑ Detailed property and equipment records are periodically balanced to the general ledger.

❑ Fixed assets are periodically appraised by an independent appraiser for insurance purposes.

❑ Detailed fixed asset records are periodically checked by physical inventory.

❑ Adequate procedures exist for the receiving and recording of gifts and fixed assets.

❑ Procedures exist governing the disposition of fixed assets.

Other

❑ Bank statement reconciliations are prepared as soon as possible after the statement is received.

❑ Bank statements are reconciled by someone other than the person(s) handling the cash receipt and cash disbursement functions.

❑ Financial statements are prepared on a timely, regular (monthly) basis and presented to appropriate board members, management, and staff for review and discussion.

❑ The financial statements format allows for comparison of actual financial activity to budgeted amounts.

❑ The organization has a fidelity insurance policy.

❑ Employee loans are prohibited.

❑ Investments are properly recorded and controlled.

❑ Procedures are in place to document the receipt of in-kind services.

❑ Minutes from board of directors meetings are prepared on a timely basis.

❑ Insurance policies are reviewed annually and provide adequate coverage.

Chapter Nine Key Concepts

- As with internal control systems designed to protect what your organization owns, systems should also be in place to safeguard your organization's expenditures and liabilities. Above all, responsibilities for the receiving and spending of resources should be separate from the financial record-keeping and reconciliation functions.

- In addition to ensuring segregation of duties for all financial transactions, your organization should also protect itself through steps such as documenting all financial policies in a manual, establishing procedures to govern the maintenance of accounting records, and maintaining an organizational chart that sets forth the actual lines of authority and responsibility. Loans to employees or board members should be strictly prohibited.

Afterword

We've come a long way in this book. We've discussed the double-entry system of bookkeeping, cash versus accrual basis accounting, posting financial transactions, creating financial statements, and developing a system of internal controls. We've looked at terms such as debits and credits, assets and liabilities, trial balances, charts of accounts, and segregation of duties.

Whether or not bookkeeping is your full-time profession, know that what you do is important. Your nonprofit needs an effective bookkeeping system to be financially astute and make wise choices and plans. Bookkeeping safeguards your organization's assets. Equally important, bookkeeping helps your nonprofit maintain financial accountability to the outside world.

It has been our privilege to take this journey with you. We hope that this book has increased your ability to track the financial activity of your nonprofit and, in so doing, contribute to the broader work of your nonprofit in the community.

Appendices

Appendix A: Accounts Payable Register

Date	Vendor/ Creditor	Vendor Account Code	Invoice Date	Invoice #	Invoice Amount	Expense Account Name	Expense Account #	Expense Account Amount	Date Paid	Amount Paid	Check #
Total All Customers											

Appendix B: Accounts Payable Subsidiary Ledger

Account #	Vendor/ Creditor Name & Address	Phone	Invoice #	Brief Description and Purpose	Date Invoice Received	Invoice Amount	Total Amount Due	0-30 Days	31-60 Days	61-90 Days	Over 90 Days
Total All Vendors											

Appendix C: Cash Disbursements Journal

Date	Payee	Check #	Invoice #	Accounts Payable Amount	Non-Accounts Payable Amount	Income Acct. Code If Non-Accts. Payable
Monthly Totals						

Appendix D: Accounts Receivable Register

Date	Customer	Customer Account Code	Invoice Date	Invoice #	Invoice Amount	Income Account Name	Income Account #
Total All Customers							

Appendix E: Accounts Receivable Subsidiary Ledger

Customer ID#	Customer Name & Address	Phone	Invoice Date	Invoice #	Invoice Follow-Up	Payments	Total Amount Due	0-30 Days	31-60 Days	61-90 Days	Over 90 Days
Total All Customers											

Appendix F: Cash Receipts Journal

Date	Received From	Customer #	Invoice #	Accounts Receivable Amount	Non-Accounts Receivable Amount	Income Acct. Code If Non-Accts. Receivable
		Monthly Totals				

Appendix G: General Journal

Date	Description of Entry	Debit	Credit

Appendix H: General Ledger

General Ledger for Account _____

Date	Description of Entry	Debit	Credit	Balance	DR or CR*

* DR = debit, CR = credit

Appendix I: Financial Summary Form

Financial Summary for _____

(Organization Name)

	Month Ending	Year-to-Date
Income		
Contributions		
Government Grants		
Earned Income		
Interest		
Other		
Subtotal		
Carryover (+/-) from Previous Year		
Total Income		
Expenses		
Personnel Costs		
Health Insurance		
FICA, Federal & State Taxes		
Rent		
All Other Expenses		
Total Expenses		
Surplus/(Deficit)		

Other Information

1. Uncollected receivables

    Less than 60 days old _____ More than 60 days old _____

2. Accounts Payable

    Less than 60 days old _____ More than 60 days old _____

3. Checking balance _____ Savings balance _____

4. Total budgeted income this year _____ % to date _____

5. Total budgeted expenses this year _____ % to date _____

6. Listing of this month's contributors: _____

    _____

7. Explanation of unusual expenses this month: _____

    _____

Appendix J: Grant Tracking Form

Grant Name: _____ Grant Number: _____

Contact:_____

Address:_____

_____

_____

_____

Phone: _____ Fax:_____

E-mail: _____

Amount: _____ Date: _____

Purpose: _____

_____

_____

_____

_____

_____

_____

Reporting Requirements: _____

_____

_____

_____

_____

_____

_____

_____

_____

_____

_____

_____

_____

Appendix K: Bank Statement Reconciliation Form

Bank Name:_____

Account Number: _____

Date of Statement: _____ _____

Ending Balance Per Bank Statement: $ _____

Add: Deposits not yet credited on statement

Date	Description	Amount
	Total Additions (+)	$

Subtract: Outstanding checks and withdrawals

Date	Description	Amount
	Total Subtractions (-)	$

Balance (should match general ledger cash account) = $ _____

Appendix L: Internal Controls Activity

This list of activities and corresponding duties will help you to apply internal control procedures discussed in Chapters Eight and Nine to your organization. It should be used in conjunction with the chart in Appendix M.

Directions:

1. Across the top of the chart, write the names of persons available to assist your organization with financial transactions.

2. For each activity on the chart, write a specific duty under the name of the person who will perform it. For example, for Incoming Cash and Checks, you might write "Open and date" under Accountant/Bookkeeper. Continue until all duties have been listed.

3. Try to achieve as much segregation of duties as possible (see Chapter Eight for more details).

I. Cash Receipts

Incoming Cash and Checks
1. Open and date
2. Record
3. Copy and deposit
4. Record in check register
5. Code for account and input into accounting

Grants Receivable
1. Open and date
2. Verify and record
3. Code for account
4. Reconcile

II. Cash Disbursements

Invoice
1. Open and match with receiving information
2. Verify invoice
3. Code for account
4. Approve
5. Input into accounting

Payment Request
1. Prepare
2. Verify
3. Code for account
4. Approve
5. Input into accounting

III. Expense Reimbursement

Invoice
1. Prepare
2. Approve
3. Verify
4. Code for account
5. Input into accounting

Generate Checks
1. Prepare
2. Record in check register
3. Obtain signature
4. Approve
5. Input into accounting

IV. Bank Reconciliation

1. Open bank statements
2. Prepare reconciliation
3. Approve and sign
4. File statement and reconciliation

Appendix L Continued

V. Payroll

Time sheet
1. Prepare
2. Sign
3. Approve
4. Submit to accountant

Payroll
1. Process
2. Obtain signature

Payroll Changes
1. Prepare
2. Approve
3. Adjust records

VI. Fixed Assets

Equipment Purchases
1. Request
2. Approve

VII. Financial Reports

1. Prepare
2. Review
3. Submit to Finance Committee and Board

VIII. Annual Budget

1. Initiate
2. Manage budget process
3. Approve final budget as presented by Finance Committee
4. Input into accounting

Appendix M: Internal Controls Activity Process Flow Chart

Activity	Executive Director:	Accountant/ Bookkeeper:	Board of Directors:
I. Cash Receipts			
Incoming Cash and Checks			
Grants Receivable			
II. Cash Disbursements			
Invoice			
Payment Request			
III. Expense Reimbursement			
Invoice			
Generate Checks			
IV. Bank Reconciliation			

Appendix M Continued

Activity	Executive Director:	Accountant/ Bookkeeper:				Board of Directors:
V. Payroll						
Time sheet						
Payroll						
Payroll Changes						
VI. Fixed Assets						
Equipment Purchases						
VII. Financial Reports						
VIII. Annual Budget						

Adapted from *Step-By-Step Bookkeeping for Tomorrow's Nonprofit: A Skill-Building Seminar of LarsonAllen Public Service Group.*
Copyright © 1998 The Stevens Group, Inc. Copyright © 2001 Larson, Allen, Weishair & Co., LLP.
All rights reserved. Used with permission.

Glossary
Terms Used in Nonprofit Accounting

Please note that some of these terms do not appear in this book. They are provided as a reference should you encounter them in the future.

Account—A record of an organization's financial transactions maintained in a special book or ledger. Separate accounts are kept for assets, liabilities, net assets, revenues, and expenses.

Account number—An assigned number that provides numerical control over accounts and provides a convenient means of referring to the account. See also chart of accounts.

Accounting—The art or system of keeping and analyzing financial records.

Accounting period—The period for which a statement of activity is customarily prepared. Examples: one month (the most common accounting period), four weeks, one quarter (of a year), twenty-six weeks, one year, fifty-two weeks.

Accounting system—A network of procedures through which financial transactions and information are accumulated, classified in an organization's accounts, recorded in the various books of account, and reported on financial statements.

Accounts payable—A liability representing the amount owed to others for services or merchandise provided to the organization.

Accounts payable register—A book or file that lists all bills and invoices owed by the organization.

Accounts payable subsidiary ledger—A book or file that lists all bills and invoices owed by the organization according to each individual organization or vendor, the total amounts of which agree with the balance of the accounts payable account in the general ledger.

Accounts receivable—An asset representing the amounts owed to the organization.

Accounts receivable register—A book or file that lists all funds owed to the organization.

Accounts receivable subsidiary ledger—A book or file that lists all bills and invoices owed to the organization according to the individual vendor or customers, the total amounts of which agree with the balance of the accounts receivable account in the general ledger.

Accrual basis accounting—An accounting system that recognizes expenses when they are incurred and revenues when they are earned, rather than when cash changes hands. It records amounts payable and amounts receivable in addition to recording transactions resulting from the exchange of cash.

Accumulated depreciation—A statement of position account that accumulates the balance of all depreciation expenses on capital or fixed assets owned by the organization.

Adjusting (journal) entry—The record made of an accounting transaction to correct an error, to reflect noncash transactions such as an accrual, write-off, provision for bad debt, or depreciation, or to otherwise bring accounts to their proper balances before financial statements are prepared.

Aging of accounts payable—The age of all amounts owed to others for services or merchandise provided to the organization.

Aging of accounts receivable—The age of all open invoices owed to an organization.

Allocate—To charge an item or group of items of revenue or cost to one or more objects, activities, processes, operations, or products using a consistent method based on a readily identifiable measure of application or consumption.

Allowance for doubtful accounts—A statement of position account that estimates the uncollectable portion of accounts receivable.

Allowance method—A method of accounting for bad debt where the value of an organization's receivables is reduced by a certain percentage each month.

Asset—A resource, object, or right of measurable financial value such as cash, securities, accounts receivable, land, buildings, or equipment.

Audit—A series of procedures followed by a professional accountant to test, on a selective basis, transactions and internal controls in effect, all with a view to forming an opinion on the fairness of the organization's annual financial statements.

Bad debt expense account—A record of the uncollectable dollar amount for services rendered for which an organization expected payment.

Balance sheet—See statement of position.

Board-designated net assets—A designation that is self-imposed by the board on a certain segment of its unrestricted net assets for some specific activity or project that is to be carried out in the future. Board designation has no legal significance.

Bookkeeping—A recording of financial transactions (including the documentation of money that flows into, out of, and throughout an organization) so their effect is shown in financial statements.

Budget—A financial plan that estimates the monetary receipts and expenditures for an operating period. Budgets may be directed toward project or program activities and are primarily used as a comparison and control feature against the actual financial results.

Capital additions—Gifts, grants, bequests, investment income, and gains on investments, restricted either permanently or for a certain time by parties outside of the organization to endowment and loan funds.

Capital assets—Assets with a relatively long useful life, such as land, buildings, or equipment. See fixed assets.

Capitalizing an asset—The process of recording the cost of land, buildings, and equipment as fixed assets, rather than expensing them when they are initially acquired.

Cash basis accounting—An accounting system that records only those events that involve the exchange of cash and ignores transactions that do not involve cash.

Cash disbursements journal—The journal recording all financial transactions involving the disbursement of cash.

Cash flow—The difference between cash receipts and disbursements over a given period.

Cash receipts journal—The journal recording financial transactions involving the receipt of cash.

Certified public accountant (CPA)—An accountant licensed by the state to certify financial statements.

Change in net assets—The difference between total income and total expenses, representing the surplus or deficit an organization has at the end of the year.

Chart of accounts—A list that organizes the agency's accounts in a systematic manner, usually by account number, to facilitate the preparation of financial statements and periodic financial reports. See also account number.

Check request—a form authorizing payment for services or merchandise provided to the organization.

Closing entries—A process by which all temporary accounts are reduced to zero; the change in net assets is determined and transferred to the unrestricted asset balance. Also called closing the books.

Closing the books—See closing entries.

Conditional promise to give—A written or oral agreement to contribute cash or other assets to another entity in which the contribution depends on the occurrence of a specified future or uncertain event to bind the promisor.

Contra-asset account—An account that reduces the value of a specific asset account; examples include allowance for doubtful accounts and accumulated depreciation.

Contributed services—Services provided at no cost to an organization. Contributed services are recognized as revenue only if they create or add value to a nonfinancial asset such as capital improvements to a building or office space; or if they require specialized skills that would typically need to be purchased if not provided by donation.

Contribution—A transfer of cash or other assets to another entity in which the transfer is unconditional, made or received voluntarily, and nonreciprocal.

Cost center—An organizational division, department, or unit having common supervision, or for which the organization wishes to collect and report income and expenses.

CPA—See certified public accountant.

Credit—See debit and credit.

Credit balance—A general ledger account with more credits than debits.

Current assets—Assets that can reasonably be expected to turn into cash or be consumed within one year.

Current liabilities—Liabilities that can reasonably be expected to be paid within one year.

Debit and credit—Technical bookkeeping terms referring to the two sides of a financial occurrence. Debit entries are listed on the left side of the ledger page and credit entries are listed on the right. The increase or decrease effect on the account depends on the type of account. The total value of debits must equal the total value of credits for any given financial occurrence.

Debit balance—A general ledger account with more debits than credits.

Debt—Borrowed funds from individuals, banks, or other institutions, generally secured with a note, which in turn may be secured by a lien against property or other assets. Ordinarily, the note states repayment and interest provisions.

Deferred revenue—Revenue received before it is earned. (For example, advance ticket sales or membership dues.)

Deficit—Expenses and losses in excess of related income; an operating loss, as refers to an accumulation of operating losses ("negative" retained income).

Depreciation expense—Accounting process to allocate the cost of capital or fixed assets to expense in a systematic and rational manner to the period the organization will benefit from the use of the asset.

Designated net assets—Unrestricted net assets set aside by action of the governing board for specific purposes. See also quasi-endowment funds, board-designated net assets.

Direct charge-off method—A method of accounting for bad debt where each receivable is evaluated on a case-by-case basis to determine the likelihood of collection; the entire amount of receivables determined to be uncollectable is charged off as bad debt.

Double-entry bookkeeping—A method of bookkeeping that recognizes a two-way, self-balancing, debit/credit entry for all financial occurrences.

Earned revenue—The amount received for goods or services delivered and for which no future liability is anticipated.

Encumbrances—Commitments in the form of orders, contracts, and similar items that will become payable when goods are delivered or services rendered. See purchase order.

Endowment—A type of donor restriction on contributed assets that stipulates that the assets endowed must remain intact either temporarily (until a stated period has passed or a specific occurrence has taken place) or permanently. The revenue earned from such assets is unrestricted unless specified otherwise by the donor or state law.

Exchange transaction—A reciprocal transfer of assets in which the resource provider receives equal or commensurate value in exchange for the transferred assets.

Exempt employee—An exempt employee is one whose job duties fall under the executive, administrative, professional, and outside sales exemptions of the Fair Labor Standards Act (FLSA). Such employees are exempt from the overtime provisions of the FLSA. (Note: The FLSA is a complex regulation; the determination of exempt employee should be discussed with an appropriate resource.) See also non-exempt employee.

Expense—Charges incurred, whether paid or unpaid, presumed to benefit the current fiscal year.

Fiduciary relationship—A relationship between persons based on trust and confidence. A fiduciary, such as a trustee, owes a duty of utmost good faith.

Financial Accounting Standards Board (FASB)—The governing board that formulates authoritative accounting standards for nongovernmental agencies. These standards, which encompass accounting rules, procedures, and applications, define accepted accounting practice and are referred to as generally accepted accounting principles (GAAP).

Fixed asset—An asset that has a relatively long useful life, usually several years or more, such as land, buildings, or equipment. See capital asset.

Functional classification—A classification of expenses that accumulates expenses according to the purpose for which costs are incurred. The primary functional classifications are program and supporting services.

Fund accounting—The process of classifying a nonprofit's resources into categories according to their nature, purpose, or restriction.

Fund balance—The previous term in the nonprofit sector for net assets, which is the difference between total assets and total liabilities.

GAAP—See generally accepted accounting principles.

General expenses—Specific costs, other than personnel costs, associated with the organization's operations, such as rent, supplies, and telephone.

General journal—A chronological listing of all financial transactions that do not appear in specific-purpose journals.

General ledger—A book or file containing individual accounts in which all the transactions from journals are summarized; this is the information that will be reported in an organization's financial statements.

Generally accepted accounting principles (GAAP)—Accounting standards for nongovernmental agencies that encompass accounting rules, procedures, and applications, and define accepted accounting practice. See also Financial Accounting Standards Board.

Grants—An unconditional promise to give assets to an organization by an individual or another organization. Grants must be recognized in the year the unconditional promise to give is received. See also multiyear grant.

Income—Assets received from contributions or revenue earned from services performed.

Income statement—See statement of activities.

Increase (decrease) in net assets—The difference between total income and total expenses representing net financial results of operations for the period. See change in net assets.

Independent contractor—An individual contracted to provide services for a business entity such that the business has the legal right to control the result of the work but does not have the legal right to control the manner and means of accomplishing the result. (Note: The determination of independent contractor status is complex and should be discussed with an appropriate resource.)

In-kind contributions—Noncash donations of voluntary services, property, equipment, or materials to which the organization can assign value.

Internal controls—The plan of organization, procedures, and records designed to enhance the safeguarding of assets and the reliability of records of an organization.

Internal financial statements—Statement of activities and statement of position produced by the organization to reflect its financial activities for a specific accounting period.

Inventory—An asset consisting of goods purchased and/or produced and held for resale.

Investment revenue—The revenue derived from the investment of assets. It includes interest, dividends, and realized and unrealized capital gains (net of losses).

Journal—A book of original entry in which all financial transactions are initially recorded. All journal entries are subsequently posted to individual accounts in the ledger.

Journal entry—An item in or prepared for a book of original entry, interpreting a business transaction in bookkeeping terms and showing the accounts to be debited and credited, together with an explanatory description of the transaction.

Ledger—A record of all transactions for an account in the chart of accounts.

Liability—A claim on the assets by an outsider representing a financial obligation. Liabilities include accounts payable, accrued expenses, and loans.

Liquid assets—Cash in banks and on hand, and other cash assets not set aside for specific purposes other than the payment of a current liability or a readily marketable investment.

Liquidity—The quality that makes an asset quickly and easily convertible into cash.

Long-term liabilities—Financial obligations that extend over a number of years.

Market value—The realizable amount for which an asset can be sold in the open market.

Modified cash basis accounting—The same as cash basis accounting except for certain items, most typically depreciation and payroll taxes, that are treated on an accrual basis. This is also known as a "hybrid method."

Multiyear grant—An unconditional promise to give grant assets to an organization by an individual or another organization that extends beyond one year. These grants must be recognized in the year the unconditional promise to give is received and must be recorded using a discount rate to measure the present value of the estimated future cash flow.

Net assets—The difference between total assets (what is owned) and total liabilities (what is owed); "net worth."

Net assets released from restrictions—The recognition that the organization has met donor-imposed restrictions for temporarily restricted net assets.

Non-exempt employee—A non-exempt employee is one whose job duties fall under the wage and overtime provisions of the Fair Labor Standards Act (FLSA). (Note: The FLSA is a complex regulation; the determination of exempt employee should be discussed with an appropriate resource.) See also exempt employee.

Noncurrent assets—Assets, such as equipment, that are not easily converted to cash and/or have a useful life of several years.

Permanent accounts—Asset, liability, and net asset accounts that accumulate financial information from the beginning of the organization to the current fiscal period; these accounts are found on the statement of position.

Permanently restricted net assets—A donor-imposed restriction that stipulates contributed assets be maintained permanently. Unless otherwise stipulated by the donor or state law, the organization is permitted to use up or expend part or all of the income derived from permanently restricted assets.

Personnel costs—Expenses relating to salaries, payroll taxes, and employee benefits.

Petty cash—A fund established to meet the minor, short-term, cash-operating needs of the organization.

Posting—The process of recording summarized journal figures to the appropriate accounts in the general ledger.

Prepaid expenses—Expenses recorded for benefits to be received in future fiscal periods.

Program services—Programs and activities carried out to fulfill the organization's mission.

Promise to give—A written or oral agreement to contribute cash or other assets to another entity. A promise to give must contain sufficient verifiable documentation that a promise was made and received.

Purchase order—A signed document authorizing a supplier to charge purchases to an organization's account and obligate the organization. See encumbrances.

Quasi-endowment funds—Unrestricted funds that the governing board of an organization, rather than a donor, has determined are to be retained and invested. The governing board has the right to decide at any time to expend the principal of such funds. See designated net assets, board-designated net assets.

Recording—The process of entering in chronological order all financial transactions into a journal.

Refundable advance—An asset that is transferred to an organization before a condition has been substantially met. Refundable advances are recorded as a liability on the statement of position until conditions are met, at which time they are recognized as revenue.

Register—See journal.

Restricted asset—An asset that has legal restrictions imposed on its use by outsiders. See temporarily restricted net assets and permanently restricted net assets.

Revenue—Assets earned or income received from services performed or goods sold.

Segregation of duties—A key component of internal controls where financial duties are assigned to individuals in a manner that ensures that no one individual can control both the recording function and the procedures relative to processing a transaction.

Single-entry bookkeeping—A method of bookkeeping that utilizes only income and expense accounts; transactions are recorded only once.

Source document—A business paper (such as a bill, invoice, receipt, check, deposit slip, or bank statement) that is the original record of a transaction and that provides information needed when accounting for the transaction.

Statement of activities—The financial statement that summarizes the financial activity of an organization for a given period. It presents the income, expenses, and changes in net assets for the period. Also known as the income statement.

Statement of cash flows—The financial statement that provides relevant information about the cash receipts and cash payments of an organization during a period.

Statement of functional expenses—The financial statement that details the specific types of expenses by object (rent, salaries, etc.) that were incurred in each of the programs and supporting activities delineated on the statement of activities.

Statement of position—The financial statement that presents an organization's financial position at a certain specified date. It lists assets, liabilities, and net assets. Also referred to as the balance sheet.

Straight line depreciation method—A depreciation method that recognizes equal amounts of depreciation over the course of an asset's useful life.

Support—Income from voluntary contributions and grants.

Support services—Auxiliary activities that provide the various support functions essential to achieve program services.

Surplus—Support and revenue in excess of expenses.

Temporarily restricted net asset—A donor-imposed restriction on contributed assets that either will eventually expire with the passage of time or will be fulfilled through action by the organization.

Temporary accounts—Income and expense accounts that accumulate financial information for one fiscal year. The accounts are closed out to zero during the year-end process of closing entries. These accounts are found on the statement of activities.

Trial balance—A listing of all accounts and their balances in the general ledger. The total of the debit amounts should equal the total of the credit amounts.

Unconditional promise to give—A "no-strings-attached" written or oral agreement to contribute cash or other assets to another entity.

Unqualified opinion—An auditor's opinion that attests to the credibility and reliability of an organization's financial statements. Also referred to as a clean opinion.

Unrealized gain (or loss)—The amount by which the market value of an asset exceeds (or is less than) the original cost of that asset.

Unrelated business income—Income generated for a nonprofit organization through an activity that is not substantially related to the purpose for which the nonprofit received tax-exempt status; the activity must be a trade or a business; and it must be regularly carried on.

Unrelated business income tax (UBIT)—A tax that nonprofit organizations are required to pay on income generated through an activity that is not substantially related to the organization's tax-exempt purpose.

Unrestricted net assets—The net asset group that contains the assets on which there are no donor restrictions and from which the bulk of financial activity is usually handled. Sometimes called operating funds or general funds.

Working capital—That portion of an organization's assets that is not invested in fixed assets, but is kept liquid to care for day-to-day working needs.

Bibliography

LarsonAllen Pubic Service Group. *If Nonprofits Counted: A Skill-Building Seminar of LarsonAllen Public Service Group.* St. Paul: LarsonAllen Public Service Group, 2001.

LarsonAllen Public Service Group. *Step-by-Step Bookkeeping for Tomorrow's Nonprofit: A Skill-Building Seminar of LarsonAllen Public Service Group.* St. Paul: LarsonAllen Public Service Group, 2001.

Stevens, Susan Kenny, and Lisa M. Anderson. *All the Way to the Bank: Smart Money Management for Tomorrow's Nonprofit.* St. Paul: The Stevens Group, 1997.

Stevens, Susan Kenny, Lisa M. Anderson, and Eric P. Stoebner. *Keeping the Books: Developing Financial Capacity in Your Nonprofit Press.* St. Paul: The Stevens Group, 1996.

Index

More results-oriented books from the Amherst H. Wilder Foundation

Finance

Bookkeeping Basics
What Every Nonprofit Bookkeeper Needs to Know
by Debra L. Ruegg and Lisa M. Venkatrathnam
Complete with step-by-step instructions, a glossary of accounting terms, detailed examples, and handy reproducible forms, this book will enable you to successfully meet the basic bookkeeping requirements of your nonprofit organization—even if you have little or no formal accounting training.
128 pages, softcover   Item # 069296

Coping with Cutbacks
The Nonprofit Guide to Success When Times Are Tight
by Emil Angelica and Vincent Hyman
Shows you practical ways to involve business, government, and other nonprofits to solve problems together. Also includes 185 cutback strategies you can put to use right away.
128 pages, softcover   Item # 069091

Financial Leadership for Nonprofit Executives
Guiding Your Organization to Long-term Success
by Jeanne Peters and Elizabeth Schaffer, CompassPoint Nonprofit Services
Provides executives with a practical guide to protecting and growing the assets of their organizations and with accomplishing as much mission as possible with those resources.
144 pages, softcover   Item # 06944X

Venture Forth! The Essential Guide to Starting a Moneymaking Business in Your Nonprofit Organization
by Rolfe Larson
The most complete guide on nonprofit business development. Building on the experience of dozens of organizations, this handbook gives you a time-tested approach for finding, testing, and launching a successful nonprofit business venture.
272 pages, softcover   Item # 069245

Management & Leadership

Benchmarking for Nonprofits
How to Measure, Manage, and Improve Results
by Jason Saul
Benchmarking—the onging process of measuring your organization against leaders—can help increase your impact, decrease your costs, impress your funders, engage your board, and sharpen your mission. This book defines a systematic and reliable way to benchmark, from preparing your organization to measuring performance and implementing best practices.
128 pages, softcover   Item # 069431

Consulting with Nonprofits: A Practitioner's Guide
by Carol A. Lukas
A step-by-step, comprehensive guide for consultants. Addresses the art of consulting, how to run your business, and much more. Also includes tips and anecdotes from thirty skilled consultants.
240 pages, softcover   Item # 069172

The Wilder Nonprofit Field Guide to
Crafting Effective Mission and Vision Statements
by Emil Angelica
Guides you through two six-step processes that result in a mission statement, vision statement, or both. Shows how a clarified mission and vision lead to more effective leadership, decisions, fundraising, and management. Includes tips, sample statements, and worksheets.
88 pages, softcover   Item # 06927X

The Wilder Nonprofit Field Guide to
Developing Effective Teams
by Beth Gilbertsen and Vijit Ramchandani
Helps you understand, start, and maintain a team. Provides tools and techniques for writing a mission statement, setting goals, conducting effective meetings, creating ground rules to manage team dynamics, making decisions in teams, creating project plans, and developing team spirit.
80 pages, softcover   Item # 069202

The Five Life Stages of Nonprofit Organizations
Where You Are, Where You're Going, and What to Expect When You Get There
by Judith Sharken Simon with J. Terence Donovan
Shows you what's "normal" for each development stage which helps you plan for transitions, stay on track, and avoid unnecessary struggles. This guide also includes The Wilder Nonprofit Life Stage Assessment to plot and understand your organization's progress in seven arenas of organization development.
128 pages, softcover   Item # 069229

The Manager's Guide to Program Evaluation:
Planning, Contracting, and Managing for Useful Results
by Paul W. Mattessich, PhD
Explains how to plan and manage an evaluation that will help identify your organization's successes, share information with key audiences, and improve services.
96 pages, softcover   Item # 069385

For current prices or to order visit us online at www.wilder.org/pubs

The Nonprofit Mergers Workbook
The Leader's Guide to Considering, Negotiating, and Executing a Merger
by David La Piana

A merger can be a daunting and complex process. Save time, money, and untold frustration with this highly practical guide that makes the process manageable and controllable. Includes case studies, decision trees, twenty-two worksheets, checklists, tips, and complete step-by-step guidance from seeking partners to writing the merger agreement, and more.

240 pages, softcover   Item # 069210

The Nonprofit Mergers Workbook Part II
Unifying the Organization after a Merger
by La Piana Associates

Once the merger agreement is signed, the question becomes: How do we make this merger work? *Part II* helps you create a comprehensive plan to achieve *integration*—bringing together people, programs, processes, and systems from two (or more) organizations into a single, unified whole.

248 pages, includes CD-ROM   Item # 069415

Nonprofit Stewardship
A Better Way to Lead Your Mission-Based Organization
by Peter C. Brinckerhoff

You may lead a not-for-profit organization, but it's not your organization. It belongs to the community it serves. You are the steward—the manager of resources that belong to someone else. The stewardship model of leadership can help your organization improve its mission capability by forcing you to keep your organization's mission foremost. It helps you make decisions that are best for the people your organization serves. In other words, stewardship helps you do more good for more people.

272 pages, softcover   Item #069423

Resolving Conflict in Nonprofit Organizations
The Leader's Guide to Finding Constructive Solutions
by Marion Peters Angelica

Helps you identify conflict, decide whether to intervene, uncover and deal with the true issues, and design and conduct a conflict resolution process. Includes exercises to learn and practice conflict resolution skills, guidance on handling unique conflicts such as harassment and discrimination, and when (and where) to seek outside help with litigation, arbitration, and mediation.

192 pages, softcover   Item # 069164

Strategic Planning Workbook for Nonprofit Organizations, Revised and Updated
by Bryan Barry

Chart a wise course for your nonprofit's future. This time-tested workbook gives you practical step-by-step guidance, real-life examples, one nonprofit's complete strategic plan, and easy-to-use worksheets.

144 pages, softcover   Item # 069075

Marketing & Fundraising

The Wilder Nonprofit Field Guide to Conducting Successful Focus Groups
by Judith Sharken Simon

Shows how to collect valuable information without a lot of money or special expertise. Using this proven technique, you'll get essential opinions and feedback to help you check out your assumptions, do better strategic planning, improve services or products, and more.

80 pages, softcover   Item # 069199

The Wilder Nonprofit Field Guide to Fundraising on the Internet
by Gary M. Grobman, Gary B. Grant, and Steve Roller

Your quick road map to using the Internet for fundraising. Shows you how to attract new donors, troll for grants, get listed on sites that assist donors, and learn more about the art of fundraising. Includes detailed reviews of 77 web sites useful to fundraisers, including foundations, charities, prospect research sites, and sites that assist donors.

64 pages, softcover   Item # 069180

Marketing Workbook for Nonprofit Organizations Volume I: Develop the Plan
by Gary J. Stern

Don't just wish for results—get them! Here's how to create a straightforward, usable marketing plan. Includes the six Ps of Marketing, how to use them effectively, a sample marketing plan, tips on using the Internet, and worksheets.

208 pages, softcover   Item # 069253

Marketing Workbook for Nonprofit Organizations Volume II: Mobilize People for Marketing Success
by Gary J. Stern

Put together a successful promotional campaign based on the most persuasive tool of all: personal contact. Learn how to mobilize your entire organization, its staff, volunteers, and supporters in a focused, one-to-one marketing campaign. Comes with *Pocket Guide for Marketing Representatives*. In it, your marketing representatives can record key campaign messages and find motivational reminders.

192 pages, softcover   Item # 069105

Funder's Guides

Community Visions, Community Solutions
Grantmaking for Comprehensive Impact
by Joseph A. Connor and Stephanie Kadel-Taras

Helps foundations, community funds, government agencies, and other grantmakers uncover a community's highest aspiration for itself, and support and sustain strategic efforts to get to workable solutions.

128 pages, softcover   Item # 06930X

For current prices, a catalog, or to order call 800-274-6024

Strengthening Nonprofit Performance
A Funder's Guide to Capacity Building
by Paul Connolly and Carol Lukas

This practical guide synthesizes the most recent capacity building practice and research into a collection of strategies, steps, and examples that you can use to get started on or improve funding to strengthen nonprofit organizations.

176 pages, softcover   Item # 069377

Other Books from Wilder

The Best of the Board Café
Hands-on Solutions for Nonprofit Boards
by Jan Masaoka, CompassPoint Nonprofit Services
232 pages, softcover   Item # 069407

Collaboration Handbook
Creating, Sustaining, and Enjoying the Journey
by Michael Winer and Karen Ray
192 pages, softcover   Item # 069032

Collaboration: What Makes It Work, 2nd Ed.
by Paul Mattessich, PhD, Marta Murray-Close, BA, and Barbara Monsey, MPH
104 pages, softcover   Item # 069326

Community Building: What Makes It Work
by Wilder Research Center
112 pages, softcover   Item # 069121

Community Economic Development Handbook
by Mihailo Temali
288 pages, softcover   Item # 069369

The Wilder Nonprofit Field Guide to
Conducting Community Forums
by Carol Lukas and Linda Hoskins
128 pages, softcover   Item # 069318

Keeping the Peace
by Marion Angelica
48 pages, softcover   Item # 860127

The Lobbying and Advocacy Handbook for Nonprofit Organizations
Shaping Public Policy at the State and Local Level
by Marcia Avner
240 pages, softcover   Item # 069261

The Nimble Collaboration
Fine-Tuning Your Collaboration for Lasting Success
by Karen Ray 136 pages, softcover
Item # 069288

The Nonprofit Board Member's Guide to Lobbying and Advocacy
by Marcia Avner
96 pages, softcover   Item # 069393

ORDERING INFORMATION

Order online, or by phone or fax

 Online: www.wilder.org/pubs
E-mail: books@wilder.org

 Call toll-free: 800-274-6024
Internationally: 651-659-6024

 Fax: 651-642-2061

Mail: Amherst H. Wilder Foundation
Publishing Center
919 Lafond Avenue
St. Paul, MN 55104

Our NO-RISK guarantee

If you aren't completely satisfied with any book for any reason, simply send it back within 30 days for a full refund.

Pricing and discounts

For current prices and discounts, please visit our web site at www.wilder.org/pubs or call toll free at 800-274-6024.

Do you have a book idea?

Wilder Publishing Center seeks manuscripts and proposals for books in the fields of nonprofit management and community development. To get a copy of our author guidelines, please call us at 800-274-6024. You can also download them from our web site at www.wilder.org/pubs/author_guide.html.

Visit us online

You'll find information about the Wilder Foundation and more details on our books, such as table of contents, pricing, discounts, endorsements, and more, at www.wilder.org/pubs.

Quality assurance

We strive to make sure that all the books we publish are helpful and easy to use. Our major workbooks are tested and critiqued by experts before being published. Their comments help shape the final book and—we trust—make it more useful to you.